FREEDOM
IN CHRIST

AUTHENTIC

SECURE

REAL

TRUSTED

FREED TO
LEAD

EFFECTIVE IDENTITY-BASED LEADERSHIP

Rod Woods and **Steve Goss**

Published by Monarch Books
an imprint of
Lion Hudson plc
Wilkinson House, Jordan Hill Road,
Oxford OX2 8DR, England
Email: monarch@lionhudson.com
www.lionhudson.com/monarch

ISBN: 978 0 85721 706 6

E-ISBN: 978 0 85721 707 3

First edition 2015
A catalogue record for this book is available from the British Library

Printed and bound in the UK, October 2015, LH26

Acknowledgments

Unless otherwise indicated, Scripture quotations are from The Holy Bible, English Standard Version® (ESV®), copyright © 2001 by Crossway, a publishing ministry of Good News Publishers. Used by permission. All rights reserved.

Contents

Contents

Welcome To *Freed To Lead*!

We are delighted that you have chosen to offer the *Freed To Lead* course. It was born out of a passion to see Christians become the great leaders God intends. We know that a company of great Christian leaders will change the world for Jesus and that God will use them to extend His loving rulership into every area of society.

Our deep desire is that this course will enable you to play your part in raising up that company of great Christian leaders, whether they exercise their leadership in the marketplace, the church, the home or some other sphere.

We also hope that it will help churches build more effective leadership teams who will in turn raise up leaders and send them out into the world to fulfil their calling.

Enjoy *Freed To Lead* and feel free to contact us if we can help you in any way as you run the course!

Please Register As A Course Leader

It costs nothing and you will receive:
* **access to a special section of the Freedom In Christ website with downloads that you will find useful when running your course.**
* **details of training available in your area.**
* **occasional news from Freedom In Christ (optional).**

Register at www.ficm.org.uk/register

We would like to take this opportunity to thank our wives, Karen Woods and Zoë Goss, for their incredible support to us on this project, specifically for their significant input to the course materials and to the smooth running of the filming process and the many pilot events we ran. You are amazing!

Format Of This Leader's Guide

For your convenience, we have divided this Leader's Guide into two sections. So that you do not also have to have a Participant's Guide, we have duplicated the Participant's Guide in the first section (pages 7 to 192). It includes the course materials and the ministry component, *The Steps To Freedom For Leaders*, and is exactly the same as the book that participants have (with the same page numbers).

The second section contains notes specifically for course leaders and starts on page 193. You will find it very helpful to read the first chapter entitled "Leading A *Freed To Lead* Course" before you begin.

A Note On Language And Spelling

As *Freed To Lead* is on sale internationally, we have consciously tried to avoid language that will not work in all English-speaking contexts. Rather than picking either American or British spellings, however, we have chosen to vary it. In the Leader's Guide and Participant's Guide we have used British spelling. In the accompanying *Freed To Lead* book we have used American spelling.

The *Freed To Lead* book: understand the principles at a deeper level

Freed To Lead by Rod Woods is the accompanying book for the course. It goes into the topics covered on the course in more depth and covers a host of related topics too. You will find it invaluable as you lead *Freed To Lead* and your course participants will appreciate it too.

Order from your local Freedom In Christ office (see page 8), the shop at www.ficm.org.uk, or www.ficm.org or your usual supplier of Christian books.

Connect With Us!

Join Rod Woods and Steve Goss on the Freed To Lead interest group on LinkedIn.
- Ask questions
- Join in discussions
- Connect with Christians in leadership

From LinkedIn, search for "Freed To Lead".

Get the Freedom In Christ Ministries app
- Daily devotional direct to your smartphone or tablet
- News and prayer requests from around the world

Search for "FICM News" at your app store.

Join the Freedom In Christ Facebook group
- Instant updates on what's happening in the world of FICM
- Share your Freedom In Christ stories

From Facebook, search for "Freedom In Christ Ministries", select the "closed group" and ask to join.

Find your local Freedom In Christ website
We operate in around 40 countries. Find your nearest office or representative at www.ficminternational.org.
- Our US site is at www.ficm.org
- Our UK site is at: www.ficm.org.uk

Register on our UK site to receive our daily devotional by email.

SESSION 1:

The Adventure Of Leadership

PARTICIPANT'S NOTES

- What is the greatest personal challenge you've faced?

- What was the outcome?

Read Psalm 37 out loud in your group, without comment.

Pause for a quiet moment of reflection on the content of the psalm.

Read

- Read 2 Timothy 1:1–14

- Read the passage again and make a list of the five most important words from the passage. Why do you think they are important?

Understand

- Who wrote this passage?

- To whom is this passage written?

- Why was this passage/letter written?

Discern

- What do you think is the gift of God that is in Timothy? (verse 6)

- What do you think it means to "fan into flame" this gift of God?

- What has God not given us? What has God given us? Why has God given us this? (verses 7–8)

Apply

- As a leader, what is the gift of God that is in you?
- What do you think you might do to "fan into flame" this gift of God?
- Why do you think Paul emphasized that God has not given us a spirit of cowardice?
- How would you describe "the spirit of cowardice"? What does it look like in leadership?
- How do power, love, and self-control counteract cowardice?
- Why are power, love, and self-control important for leaders?
- In light of this passage, what might you expect as a leader – both positively and negatively?

Commit

- In your leadership, when have you experienced "the spirit of cowardice"? Why? What did you do when you were faced with this cowardice?
- In light of this passage, what might you do as a leader when faced with cowardice?

Purpose Of *Freed To Lead*

To enable Christians to lead confidently from a vision of Christian leadership based on our identity in Christ.

Pause For Thought

Throughout this course, we will give you many opportunities to discuss your own thoughts and ideas about leadership. When we use the word "leadership", we all assume that we know what we're talking about. So let's consider the following questions:

What is "leadership"?

What makes a good leader?

Which of the two questions was more difficult to answer? Why?

The Bible And Leadership

The Bible is our foundation for understanding leadership.

In *Freed To Lead* we will **not** reduce Jesus or the Bible to

- a set of principles
- a private morality
- a surface covering of worldly styles of leadership.

Christian leadership is <u>the</u> leadership the world really needs today – not just the Church.

Leadership Is Tough

For this reason I remind you to fan into flame the gift of God, which is in you through the laying on of my hands, for God has not given us a spirit of cowardice (that comes from anxiety) but of power and of love and of self-control.

(2 Timothy 1:6–7, our own translation)

Why Is It So Difficult To Lead – Especially For Christians?

Leaders feel like failures

No adventure is easy – adventures test our stamina and courage

Struggles in leadership do not indicate that something is wrong with you

But understand this, that in the last days there will come times of difficulty.

2 Timothy 3:1

Why Leadership Is Tough

People are **overwhelmed by**

- Change
- Challenges
- Choices

People are **overloaded**

- Information overload
- Choice overload

People are **unfocused**

- Without a coherent worldview
- Without a strong set of values
- Without a focus

People are **undisciplined**

- Lawlessness
- Changing morality

People are **anxious**

- Broken society
- Unstable
- Hopeless, expecting loss

Leaders feel **disempowered** and **demoralized.**

The Leadership Dilemma

In each session we will consider a "Leadership Dilemma".
A dilemma is a challenge with no straightforward solution.

Our society needs real, effective leadership. Such leadership is the only way we can resolve the great issues of our times, whether they are personal, social, economic, or global. Yet the very people who need true leadership are the ones who consciously or unconsciously undermine, attack, sabotage, and destroy leadership.

Pause For Thought

Take a moment to review your own perspectives about the times in which we live as leaders. Discuss the following questions:

Do you agree that it is difficult to be a leader today? Why or why not?

Have you experienced resistance to your leadership? What effect has this had on you?

As a leader, do you generally feel encouraged or discouraged? Why?

The Message Of Freedom In Christ

Know the **truth** of who you are in Christ:

>A saint – a holy one

>Significant

>Accepted

>Secure.

Be aware of the reality of the spiritual world and resolve spiritual issues with **truth.**

Be transformed through the renewing of your mind with **truth.**

As Christians, we have a great leadership advantage. Jesus Christ, the greatest leader who ever lived, lives in us by the power of the Holy Spirit. Jesus has destroyed the power of sin, death, and hell in the cross and the empty tomb.

WALK IT OUT

What action(s) will you take in the coming week to apply what you have learned?

Pray for those who are feeling discouraged as leaders.

Pray for one another's leadership challenges.

For further information on the topics covered in this session, see the accompanying book, *Freed To Lead*, by Rod Woods, chapters 1 and 2.

Your Leadership Journey

Throughout *Freed To Lead* you are encouraged to create a timeline of your leadership experiences. The purpose is to help you reflect on your leadership experiences – both positive and negative – so that the concepts presented in the course can be applied to your leadership context.

You can complete your timeline on the next page. If you need more space to write, simply copy it out onto a separate sheet of paper.

At this point, record your first experiences of leadership – at school, at church, in sports, in family life.

Progress to your first "professional" or "official" position of leadership – first job, position at church, leading a club or team.

Who were influential leaders you followed as you were developing as a leader?

You will come back to do more work on the timeline in future sessions of *Freed To Lead*.

First experiences of leadership

Influential leaders

First "official" position of leadership

Memorable successes

Subsequent positions of leadership

Times of conflict or disappointment

Current position of leadership

Hopes and dreams for this position

Who do you lead?

Signs of the health of your system

Periods of personal anxiety

What do you do?

Periods of systemic anxiety

Who are you as a leader?

Potential pitfalls

Potential future position?

Goals to transform your leadership

WELCOME

- Who would you consider to be the greatest leader in all of history?
- Why?

WORSHIP

Read Psalm 37:1–4.

Express your trust in the Lord. Praise God by expressing His goodness and delightfulness.

WORD

Read

Read Luke 22:24–27, John 20:19–23, Luke 12:42–48, John 10:10–15, Galatians 4:1–7.

Understand

Create a one or two word title for each passage. Write it under the reference in the chart below.

Discern

For each passage make a comparison – what does the passage say about Jesus? What does the passage say about the disciples/us?

	What does it say about **Jesus**?	What does it say about **us**?
Luke 22:24–27		
John 20:19–23		
Luke 12:42–48		
John 10:10–15		
Galatians 4:1–7		

Apply

- What do all five passages have in common?
- Based on these passages, in what ways are we like Jesus? In what ways are we different?

Commit

- Which metaphor best describes your current style of leadership?
- Which metaphor might reveal a weakness or lack in your leadership?

In light of these passages write a list of statements about who you are because of who Jesus is, for example, "Because Jesus was with us as one who serves, I am like the least, as one who serves."

Every single one of us can be a real Christ-centred leader. In this session we will consider the nature of true Christian leadership and what makes it distinctively different from other forms of leadership.

Pause For Thought

We will start by considering a key question when it comes to leadership.

"Leaders are born, not made." What do you think about this statement? What does the Bible have to say about it?

Our response to the statement will say a lot about how we understand leadership in general and Christian leadership in particular.

The Nature Of Real Christian Leadership

Servant: *A dispute also arose among them, as to which of them was to be regarded as the greatest. And he said to them, "The kings of the Gentiles exercise lordship over them, and those in authority over them are called benefactors. But not so with you. Rather, let the greatest among you become as the youngest, and the leader as one who serves. For who is the greater, one who reclines at table or one who serves? Is it not the one who reclines at table? But I am among you as one who serves."*

Luke 22:24–27

Sent One: *Jesus said to them again, "Peace be with you. As the Father has sent me, even so I am sending you."*

John 20:21

Steward: And the Lord said, "Who then is the faithful and wise manager, whom his master will set over his household, to give them their portion of food at the proper time?"

Luke 12:42

Shepherd: He who is a hired hand and not a shepherd, who does not own the sheep, sees the wolf coming and leaves the sheep and flees, and the wolf snatches them and scatters them.

John 10:12

Son: So you are no longer a slave, but a son, and if a son, then an heir through God.

Galatians 4:7

Real Christian Leaders:

- Are followers
  "Follow me, and I will make you fishers of men." Matthew 4:19

- Believe that the Bible is the Word of God and live accordingly

- Have a genuine relationship with God

- Are grounded in the reality of who they now are in Christ

- Are being led by the Spirit of God and growing in the fruit of the Spirit

- Are becoming more and more like Jesus in character.

Christian leadership is an issue of discipleship. If we are not following Jesus well, we won't lead others well.

Christian Leadership Is:

the interactive relational process

of influencing people and people-systems

towards beneficial outcomes

through

   your identity,

   character, and

   calling in Christ,

using

   your God-given strengths

   and spiritual gifts

as well as

   your talents,

   skills, and knowledge.

The Definition "Unpacked"

Process – ongoing, never fully complete

Relational – people-centred, not task-oriented

Interactive – expect to be changed, not just to change others

Influencing both people and people-systems – individuals as well as groups and organizations

Outcomes – the "fruit"

- Economic
- Social
- Environmental
- Personal
- Spiritual

Identity – who you are in Christ

People will follow who you are and how you are before they will follow what you do or say.

Strengths and spiritual gifts – God has called you and supernaturally, uniquely gifted you.

Are leaders born or made? The answer is both!

Talents, skills, knowledge – leadership is not only **who you are** but also **what you do**.

Excellence in leadership demands focus on your strengths and delegation in your "weaknesses."

Definition Of Christian Leadership

Christian leadership is the interactive relational process of influencing people and people-systems towards beneficial outcomes through your identity, character, and calling in Christ, using your God-given strengths and spiritual gifts as well as your talents, skills, and knowledge.

Pause For Thought

So we are called to lead, whether or not we are a "natural" leader! Discuss the following questions:

How has this session challenged or changed your perception of leadership?

What has been the most important concept for you in this session and why?

How does "Christian" leadership differ from the world's understanding of leadership?

The Leadership Dilemma

We tend to think that becoming a better leader is all about improving our leadership style or trying to look like what we think a "natural" leader looks like. However, those are not the things that will make us great leaders.

Real Christian leadership can transform society. It is the type of leadership that every organization everywhere needs.

Our vision is to see genuinely Christian leadership not just in homes and churches but all over the place, to see Christians being so obviously great leaders that they are in demand everywhere.

WALK IT OUT

What was the outcome of your action item(s) from the last session?

How will you apply what you have learned during the coming week?

Pray for one another to become the leaders God desires.

Reflect on your own leadership experiences using the leadership timeline on page 18:

- What memorable experiences and successes do you recall from your past leadership?
- What conflicts and/or disappointments arose in those past experiences of leadership?

You will be encouraged to work through *The Steps to Freedom For Leaders* at the end of this course. But if something in this session has prompted you to want to examine your identity as a leader more closely, you might like to look at Steps 1 and 2 now (pages 138–150).

> For further information on the topics covered in this session, see the accompanying book, *Freed To Lead*, by Rod Woods, chapter 3.

How To Connect With Freedom In Christ's Discipleship Teaching

You don't have to have gone through Freedom In Christ's core teaching to do *Freed To Lead* but it helps. Here are some ways you can get to grips with it:

Victory Over The Darkness and *The Bondage Breaker* were written by Neil Anderson, the founder of Freedom In Christ, and contain the core message.

The Freedom In Christ Course by Neil Anderson and Steve Goss has been used by over 250,000 people around the world.

Steve Goss wrote *The Discipleship Series*, four concise, straightforward books that contain the message of *The Freedom In Christ Course*. Their titles are: *Free To Be Yourself*; *Win The Daily Battle*; *Break Free, Stay Free*; and *The You God Planned*.

The Grace Course by Steve Goss, Rich Miller, and Jude Graham contains the core message of Freedom In Christ with an emphasis on understanding the grace of God in our hearts not just our heads.

The Steps To Freedom In Christ by Neil Anderson is the ministry component of our core teaching. A kind and gentle way to get rid of "rubbish" from the past, it has been used by millions around the world.

Get further information at www.ficm.org.uk or from your local Freedom In Christ office or representative (see page 8).

SESSION 3:

Being And Doing

PARTICIPANT'S NOTES

- If you had a chance for a "makeover" in life, what would you do differently?

WORSHIP

Read Psalm 37:5-8.

Wait silently before the Lord for several minutes.

Thank God that He will act on your behalf and that he will make your righteousness and justice shine.

WORD

Read

Read Galatians 5:13-26, Luke 6:43-45.

Understand

- Who wrote the passage from Galatians? To whom was it written?
- Why was this passage/letter written?
- Who is speaking in the Luke passage?

Discern

- What is the opposite of "the Spirit?"

Make a comparison chart on the following page by listing the fruit of the Spirit and the work of its opposite.

The Spirit	The _____

- According to Galatians 5, what is your calling?

Apply

Compare and contrast the theme of the passage in Luke with the passage
in Galatians:

- How are the themes of the passages different? How are they the
  same?
- Why are the "works of the flesh" like "devouring" one another?
- How do you "walk by the Spirit?" Why is it important to "walk by the
  Spirit?"
- Where does "good fruit" come from? How do you cultivate "good
  fruit"?

Commit

- Do you think leaders are more or less likely to give in to the flesh?
- When have you given in to the works of the flesh? What keeps you
  from walking in the Spirit? Ask God for forgiveness and commit to a
  pattern of walking in the Spirit.
- What are the treasures of your heart? How have they produced good
  fruit in your leadership?

We are wired to "do" and we naturally assume that our behaviour is the primary issue. Yet the primary issue in both discipleship and leadership is not doing: it's being.

Pause For Thought

We tend to learn a lot from other leaders, especially those we have followed ourselves. They can make an indelible mark on our lives.

What is the best experience you've had with a leader?
Why was it so good?

The Pharisees' Leadership – A Focus On "Doing"

"Do you not see that whatever goes into the mouth passes into the stomach and is expelled? But what comes out of the mouth proceeds from the heart, and this defiles a person. For out of the heart come evil thoughts, murder, adultery, sexual immorality, theft, false witness, slander. These are what defile a person. But to eat with unwashed hands does not defile anyone."

Matthew 15:17–20

"They are blind guides. And if the blind lead the blind, both will fall into a pit."

Matthew 15:14

Your doing will always flow from your being.

BEING
Identity, Character, Calling

A unique person

- Mind
- Will
- Emotions

A unique temperament

- Introvert or Extrovert
- Thinker or Feeler

A unique background

- Culture
- Gender
- Upbringing
- Experiences

A unique make-up

- Natural abilities
- Strengths
- Weaknesses

DOING
Actions, Choices

Making choices

Taking action

Building relationships

All leadership involves both who you are and what you do. If your being is not right, your doing will not lead in a healthy way.

The Advantage Of Being A Christian Leader

BEING
A New Creation

Holy

The righteousness of God

Completely forgiven

Accepted

Pleasing to God

Full of the Holy Spirit

DOING
Actions, Choices

Making choices

Taking action

Building relationships

If your being is right, your doing will lead in a healthy way.

Enemies Of Real Christian Leadership

The World Can Hold Us Back

The world encourages us to look to our status or position to get our sense of worth.

To the degree that we base our identity in our leadership position, our leadership will be distorted, dysfunctional, or less effective.

People will follow **who you are** and **how you are** before they will follow what you do or what you say.

God is not measuring you by your job level, the size of the team you lead, the outward trappings of success, or any other external factor. He has just one concern: your character – whether or not you are becoming more and more like Jesus.

The Devil Can Hold Us Back

"In your anger do not sin": do not let the sun go down while you are still angry, and do not give the devil a foothold.

Ephesians 4:26

I gave you milk, not solid food, for you were not yet ready for it [literally: able to receive it]... since there is jealousy and quarrelling among you.

1 Corinthians 3:2

The Bible is clear that when we sin we give the enemy a **foothold** in our lives, a place from which to operate.

The battleground is our mind, our thinking.

Submit yourselves, then, to God. Resist the devil, and he will flee from you.

James 4:7

The Steps To Freedom In Christ (see page 30) is a process to help you remove the footholds of the enemy and ensure that your being is healthy.

The Flesh Can Hold Us Back

We can try to lead in our own strength – thinking the outcome depends on us. We'll become angry and frustrated as we fail and blame ourselves or other people.

The key issue is knowing what is really true and making a choice, moment by moment.

Live by the Spirit and you will not gratify the desires of the flesh.

Galatians 5:16

Do not be conformed to this world, but be transformed by the renewal of your mind.

Romans 12:2a

We must make a habit of renewing our mind, uncovering the lies we are prone to believe and replacing them with truth.

Stronghold-Busting

Determine the lie you have come to believe

What effect has believing it had in your life?

Find as many Bible verses as you can that state the truth and write them down.

Write a prayer/declaration

- I renounce the lie that...
- I announce the truth that...

Read the Bible verses and say the prayer/declaration daily for 40 days.

Character Is The Key

Leadership is essentially a discipleship process.

A disciple is "someone who is learning to become more and more like Jesus in character."

The evidence of growing in character is an increase in the fruit of the Spirit in your life that will show in your actions.

> *But the fruit of the Spirit is*
>
> > *love,*
> >
> > *joy,*
> >
> > *peace,*
> >
> > *patience,*
> >
> > *kindness,*
> >
> > *goodness,*
> >
> > *faithfulness,*
> >
> > *gentleness,*
> >
> > *self-control;*
>
> *against such things there is no law.*
>
> *Galatians 5:22–23*

Maturity is:

- an increase in willingness to take responsibility for your own mind, will, and emotions (soul) and make good choices
- an increase of love for others and a want to serve them in humility
- an increase in consistency between the internal and external – "what you see is what you get" – that others will experience as integrity.

Brokenness And Fruitfulness

> *So to keep me [Paul] from becoming conceited because of the surpassing greatness of the revelations, a thorn was given me in the flesh, a messenger of Satan to harass me, to keep me from becoming conceited. Three times I pleaded with the Lord about this, that it should leave me. But he said to me,* **"My grace is sufficient for you, for my power is made perfect in weakness."** *Therefore I will boast all the more gladly of my weaknesses, so that the power of Christ may rest upon me. For the sake of Christ, then, I am content with weaknesses, insults, hardships, persecutions, and calamities. For when I am weak, then I am strong.*
>
> *2 Corinthians 12:7–10*

Part of God's preparation for real Christian leaders is brokenness.

We never experience the power of God in our lives unless we are brought to "an end of ourselves."

God might use:

- Loss of reputation
- Personal conflict
- Injustice
- Health issues
- Financial difficulties.

His purposes are:

- To get to the issues needing to be resolved
- To move us to the place of knowing that we are dependent on Him
- To strip away those things which we have made to be substitutes for God
- To restore the intimacy of our relationship with Him.

Leadership Also Involves Doing

All leadership involves both who you are and what you do. Your doing flows from your being – ALWAYS!

Deciding

- Acting in faith
- Making the choice.

Discerning

- Recognizing God's best for people and people-systems.

Directing

- Giving vision and mission
- Keeping an eye on the big picture.

Developing

- Promoting health in people and systems.

Delegating

- Sharing authority with responsibility.

Disciplining

- Creating shape and form
- Training with focus and correcting behaviour if necessary.

Criteria When Considering A Leadership Style Or Theory:

- Is it consistent with the Bible?
- Does it flow from the leader's being?
- Is it appropriate and beneficial for the context and situation?
- Is it wise?

The Leadership Dilemma

Jesus said: *"I can do nothing on my own."*	Paul said: *"I can do all things through him who strengthens me."*
John 5:30	Philippians 4:13

We can have a tendency either to forge ahead and do things in our strength or to hang back too much and not do what we should. The biblical principle is: I can do "all things" but only "through him who strengthens me".

Pause For Thought

In this session, we have introduced a concept that may be new to you: how our being as leaders shapes our leadership.

How do you understand the difference between being and doing in leadership?

How important do you think your "style" of leadership is? Why?

How has the world, the flesh, or the devil held you back in leadership? How will you overcome this?

WALK IT OUT

What was the outcome of your action item(s) from the last session?

How will you apply what you have learned this week?

Pray for one another in your leadership responsibilities.

Reflect on your own leadership experiences using the leadership timeline on page 18:

- Describe your current leadership position. Who are you as a leader? What do you do? Who do you lead?

- What are your hopes and dreams? What are signs of health in your context?

For further information on the topics covered in this session, see the accompanying book, *Freed To Lead*, by Rod Woods, chapters 4 and 5.

SESSION 4:

Leading In Your Context

PARTICIPANT'S NOTES

Which Old Testament person do you most identify with? Why?

Read Psalm 37:9–13.

Thank God that wickedness and wrongdoing shall not prevail.

Thank God that His people will inherit the land – that is, become people of influence throughout your city, region, or nation.

Read

Read 1 Corinthians 12:12–31.

As you read, make note of the words "one" and "many" or "all".

Understand

- Who wrote this passage?
- To whom is this passage written?
- Why was this passage/letter written?

Discern

- Metaphorically, in this passage what does "the body" represent?
- What do the "parts of the body" represent?
- Which parts of the body are given greater honour?
- Why do you think God has made the body in this way?
- How does the suffering of one member of the body affect the whole body?
- How does the honouring of one member affect the whole body?

Apply

- How would you describe the corporate culture of the Corinthian church?
- What things tend to affect "the body" both positively and negatively?
- Describe what it feels like to have a blister on your foot. How does it affect the way you walk? What do you think might be the spiritual equivalent of having a "blister" on your "walk"?
- What is the spiritual equivalent of having a "blister" on the body of Christ?
- Describe a time when someone under your leadership was suffering. How did the group suffer? How did you suffer?
- What do you think would be the effect of "a member" being separated from "the body"? How would this affect the individual member? How would this affect the body?

Commit

- Describe a way that you could honour another part of the body to which you belong. How do you think this might affect the whole body?
- When have you felt separated from "the body"? What were the circumstances surrounding this? How did it affect the group you lead?
- How can you reconnect to the body?

A leader who has been successful in one place can fail in another leadership context – and vice versa.

> **Pause For Thought**
>
> Sometimes it seems that leadership is a mystery. We simply don't know why we might seem to succeed one time and then seem to fail another time.
>
> When do you find it easiest to lead?
> When do you find it difficult to lead?
> What makes the most difference between the two?

People-Systems

System: a set of things working together as parts of a complex whole.

- A computer system
- A digestive system

People-system: a set (group) of people with a connectedness from which its own identity and form emerge. It develops a common sense of identity and way of doing things.

- The human family
- The biblical term "household"

Why People-Systems

People-systems always influence the behaviours of the people within them. They govern :

- Organization, identity, and ways of relating
- Personal satisfaction and meaning
- Conforming behaviour

> **People-systems will influence us even more than we influence them.**

Leaders In People-Systems

The biblical word for leaders of people-systems is "**steward**".

All people-systems have leaders. Some form of leadership will always emerge.

- If we behave like a leader and people follow, we are leading, regardless of our title.
- If people do **not** see us as leader or do **not** follow, we are **not** leading, regardless of our title.

People-Systems As "Persons"

Brain

The leader is like **the brain.**

- Through our *being* we regulate healthy functioning of the people-system.
- Through our *doing* we help the people-system make good choices and take wise actions.

Our *being* as leaders influences our people-systems more deeply and profoundly than we realize. It is our primary leadership influence in our people-system.

Spirit

The **spirit** of a people-system: an invisible reality which influences and affects people within its range socially and spiritually.

The spirit of a people-system operates in accordance with spiritual principles:

- Sin and legalism bring death to the spirit of the people-system.
- Repentance and forgiveness bring life to the spirit of the people-system.
- If we sow to the flesh in a people-system, we will reap corruption.
- If we sow to the spirit in a people-system, we reap life in the people-system.

The past influences the present in the people-system.

Soul

The **soul** of a people-system: the emotions, the mind, and the will.

- Emotions or "emotional processes" of a people-system are:

    The complex interplay of

    - Impressions
    - Feelings – especially liking and disliking

    All of which influence

    - Thoughts
    - Emotions
    - Choices.

- The mind of a people-system: the thinking processes and attitudes.

- The will of a people-system: making corporate choices and decisions.

Body

The "flesh and bones" of a people-system:

- Structures such as buildings
- Policies and procedures such as constitutions
- The ways it portrays itself such as websites
- How members of the people-system interface with one another such as small groups.

The body of a people-system is the expression of the interplay of the spirit, soul, and brain (leadership) of the people-system.

A great mistake is to assume that we can lead by first changing the **body** *of a people-system rather than by promoting health and positive change in the* **spirit** *and* **soul** *of the people-system.*

Pause For Thought

The idea of people-systems might be a completely new concept to you, but you will certainly have experienced their influence.

How have you experienced the influence of people-systems in your life and in your leadership?
When have you seen effective leadership in a people-system?
When have you seen a people-system destroy good leadership?

The Leadership Dilemma

Becoming a healthy leader is one of our greatest responsibilities. Yet being a healthy leader alone does not determine our fruitfulness as a leader. A healthy people-system will often help make an unhealthy leader effective; an unhealthy people-system will often render a healthy leader ineffective. This means that our people-system will determine our leadership effectiveness far more than we realize.

What was the outcome of your action item(s) from the last session?

How will you apply what you have learned this week?

Pray for one another in your leadership responsibilities.

For further information on the topics covered in this session, see the accompanying book, *Freed To Lead*, by Rod Woods, chapter 6.

Setting Your Ministry Free

Nothing takes the wind out of a church's or ministry's sails more than dysfunctional leadership, internal strife, unresolved conflict, and unresolved sin from the past. Freedom In Christ Ministries regularly facilitates retreats for church and ministry leadership teams to resolve these issues.

Leaders report significant breakthroughs, an end to repeating patterns of division and other sins, and a new sense of unity.

The retreats are based on the process outlined in *Setting Your Church Free* or *Extreme Church Makeover* by Neil Anderson and Charles Mylander.

This is a process of establishing the healthy leadership patterns needed to guide a Spirit-led process of renewal and refocusing. During the process leadership teams address corporate sins, spiritual attacks, and destructive corporate mindsets. They finish by putting together a Prayer Action Plan that guides them as they seek to apply what God shows them during the retreat during the following weeks and months.

For further information contact your local Freedom In Christ representative (see page 8).

Building Healthy People-Systems

What does a perfect day look like to you?

Read Psalm 37:14–16.

Thank God for how He cares for the poor and needy and how He provides for His people.

Read

Read Colossians 3:2–17.

- What are the things that we are encouraged to do ourselves?
- What are the things that we are encouraged to allow someone else to do in us or for us?

Understand

- Who wrote this passage?
- To whom is it written?
- What is the main theme of this passage?

Discern

- How does Paul describe the people to whom he is writing?
- What does Paul say to the people to "put on" or "let dwell within" you?
- What does Paul say to the people they should do?
- How should these things be done?
- Why should they be done?

Apply

- How do the traits which we are to "put on" or "let dwell within" become a part of us?
- How do these traits affect you as a leader?
- How do these traits in you affect the group you lead?

Commit

- When is it most difficult to demonstrate the traits described in this passage in your own life?
- What actions might increase your ability to "put on" the traits to which Paul refers?
- What attitudes increase your ability to exercise these traits in your leadership – both your attitudes and the attitudes of those you lead?

Healthy People-Systems

Without healthy leadership, it's impossible for an unhealthy people-system to become healthy.

Leadership is the primary determinant of whether people-systems remain healthy or become even more fruitful.

Three hallmarks of healthy leaders:

1. Having our being grounded in Jesus
2. Genuine humility – a sober, truth-filled view of ourselves and a knowledge of the greatness of God
3. Holy determination – perseverance.

Pause For Thought

We've talked a lot about what makes a good leader. Sometimes it's helpful to learn from the opposite example. We can learn what not to do in leadership and discover what can make our leadership ineffective.

What makes a bad leader?
What disrupts effective leadership?
How do you know when a people-system is healthy?

Three characteristics of healthy people-systems:

1. Mutual submission

Submit to one another out of reverence for Christ.
Ephesians 5:21

2. Unity

Behold, how good and pleasant it is when brothers dwell in unity! It is like the precious oil on the head, running down on the beard, on the beard of Aaron, running down on the collar of his robes! It is like the dew of Hermon, which falls on the mountains of Zion! For there the LORD has commanded the blessing, life forevermore.

Psalm 133

I therefore, a prisoner for the Lord, urge you to walk in a manner worthy of the calling to which you have been called, with all humility and gentleness, with patience, bearing with one another in love, eager to maintain the unity of the Spirit in the bond of peace. There is one body and one Spirit – just as you were called to the one hope that belongs to your call – one Lord, one faith, one baptism, one God and Father of all, who is over all and through all and in all.

Ephesians 4:1–6

I appeal to you, brothers, by the name of our Lord Jesus Christ, that all of you agree, and that there be no divisions among you, but that you be united in the same mind and the same judgment.

1 Corinthians 1:10

3. Love

And above all these put on love, which binds everything together in perfect harmony.

Colossians 3:14

Unhealthy People-Systems

Three characteristics of dysfunctional people-systems:

1. Rebelliousness – refusing to co-operate; making demands
2. Factionalism – secrets, gossip and rumours
3. Selfism – a radical sense of selfishness.

Building Healthy People-Systems

The power to influence our people-system towards health flows from *our being*:

- Our own spiritual health – significance, security, and acceptance grounded in Jesus Christ
- Our genuine and authentic commitment to our people – a tangible loving presence in their midst.

In most marriages, the husband and wife commit to one another "in sickness and in health". If we are to have a lasting influence in our people-systems as leaders, we must also commit ourselves to them in sickness and in health.

The Bane Of Leadership – Anxiety

Anxiety: the painful and disturbing unease or apprehension that stems from inappropriate concern about something uncertain.

- Acute anxiety – episodic.
- Chronic anxiety – ongoing, persistent, habitual.

Anxiety In The Bible

...for God gave us a spirit not of fear but of power and love and self-control.

2 Timothy 1:7

Fear: "cowardice or failure of nerve that comes from anxiety".

Humble yourselves, therefore, under the mighty hand of God so that at the proper time he may exalt you, casting all your anxieties on him, because he cares for you. Be sober-minded; be watchful. Your adversary the devil prowls around like a roaring lion, seeking someone to devour. Resist him, firm in your faith, knowing that the same kinds of suffering are being experienced by your brotherhood throughout the world.

1 Peter 5:6–9

This passage shows a connection between anxiety and the demonic – anxiety makes Christians susceptible to demonic attack.

"Anxiety" can also be translated as "concern" or "care." It describes an emotional state that causes us to attach importance to something. Like anger, it indicates that something needs to be addressed.

Roots Of Anxiety

- Identity and integrity not grounded in Jesus Christ.
- Lost and ungrounded – lacking confidence.
- Overloaded and confused.
- Loss aversion.
- Idolatry (trusting people and things rather than God).
- Not taking appropriate responsibility.

Features Of Anxiety

1. Anxiety is infectious.
2. Anxiety disguises itself.
3. Anxiety distorts everything in a person and a people-system.
4. Anxiety weakens the natural defences of people and people-systems – both become susceptible to the influence of outside forces.
5. Anxiety is resistible.

Anxiety And The Demonic

Anxiety is a spiritual dynamic as well as an emotional dynamic. Demons, including principalities and powers, seek to produce and magnify anxiety in people and people-systems in order to control them. Left unresolved, anxiety will give a foothold for the demonic in any person or people-system.

Recognizing Anxiety

Symptoms Of Anxiety In **People**	Symptoms Of Anxiety In **People-Systems**
• Loss of imagination • Inability to reason • Inability to choose • Emotionality • Distorted communication • Defensiveness • "Too much" syndrome – too much food, alcohol, TV, etc • Seeking quick fixes • Restlessness • Helplessness	• Intolerance of pain • Adjusting to immaturity and irresponsibility • Preoccupation with comfort and convenience • Fad issues and cures • Corporate self-centredness • Focusing on rights • Obsession with rules • Exaggeration • Vague, ill-defined complaints • Groupthink
Chronic Anxiety in **People** • Wilfulness • Self-centredness • Fault-finding and criticism • Blame-shifting • Harmful behaviours	Chronic Anxiety in **People-Systems** • Fixate on what they perceive to be the problem • Gather in factions • Fixate on peripheral issues such as health and safety • Develop unrealistic expectations • Attacking one another personally, especially leaders

Static In Communication

When anxiety is present in a person or a system, it always hinders good communication.

Anxiety Producers In Communication	Anxiety Reducers In Communication
• Anger • Emotionality • Rumours and secrets (even when people don't know about them) • Complaining and grumbling	• Being calm and gentle • Being hopeful • Having transparency and openness • Smiling • Listening actively • Moderating your speech and tone • Sincere praise and thanksgiving • Embracing pain in yourself and others

To the degree that we have unmanaged or unresolved anxiety, we cannot lead effectively. Anxiety in the leader always produces or magnifies anxiety in the people-system.

For further reading on anxiety we recommend
A Failure Of Nerve by Edwin H. Friedman (Seabury Books, 2007).

Pause For Thought

We often fail to consider how the health of our people-system influences our leadership effectiveness.

Based on what you have learned in this session, how would you evaluate the current health of the people-system you lead?

How have you seen the effects of anxiety in your life, your leadership, or the people-systems you are part of?

What other sicknesses have you seen influence people-systems? How did you overcome those sicknesses?

The Leadership Dilemma

True leadership is the only way we have of resolving chronic anxiety, whether in people or people-systems. Yet true leadership often intensifies anxiety before leading people and people-systems out of anxiety. Things can seem to get much worse before they get better.

With your being grounded in Christ and your doing flowing from your being you *can* lead your people-system to health.

What was the outcome of your action item(s) from the last session?

How will you apply what you have learned this week?

Pray for the health of each people-system represented in your group.

For further information on the topics covered in this session, see the accompanying book, *Freed To Lead*, by Rod Woods, chapters 6 and 9.

Overcoming Personal Anxiety

WELCOME

What was your most embarrassing moment?

WORSHIP

Read Psalm 37:17–20.

Thank and praise God for how He cares for, protects, and provides for His people during difficult times.

WORD

Read

Read 1 Peter 5:6–11.

Read the passage again and note every promise from God in the passage. Note whether the promises are conditional or unconditional. What might keep us from receiving the promises?

Understand

- Who wrote this passage?
- To whom is this passage written?
- Why was this passage/letter written?

Discern

- What does this passage teach us about the person and nature of God?
- What do you think it means to humble ourselves?

- What are anxieties? What do you think it means to cast all our anxieties on God?
- What do you think it means for the devil to "prowl around like a roaring lion"? What would that look like in practice?
- What would it look like for the devil to "devour" someone?
- What does God promise in verse 10? What do you think each promise means?
- What is the significance of Peter's declaration in verse 11?

Apply

- What is the "proper time" to which Peter refers (verse 6)? How would we recognize it?
- What do you think it means to resist the devil? How might we do this?
- How does knowing that other Christians are experiencing the same kinds of suffering help us to be firm in our faith?
- What characteristics or activities of God mentioned by Peter might comfort and encourage us?
- What is the role or purpose of suffering (verses 9–10) in this passage?
- How have you experienced each of God's promises in verse 10 in your life in the past?
- In light of this passage, what might you expect as a leader – both positively and negatively?

Commit

- What would it look like for you as a leader to cast all your anxieties on God?
- How might you be sober-minded and watchful regarding your leadership?

Anxiety in a man's heart weights him down, but a good word makes him glad.

Proverbs 12:25

Therefore do not be anxious about tomorrow, for tomorrow will be anxious for itself. Sufficient for the day is its own trouble.

Matthew 6:34

Do not be anxious about anything, but in everything by prayer and supplication with thanksgiving let your requests be made known to God.

Philippians 4:6

Anxiety Definition

The painful and disturbing

unease or apprehension

that stems from

inappropriate

concern

about something uncertain.

> Concern is a natural emotion. It's an indicator that something is important to you. Not all concern is inappropriate.
>
> Appropriate concern comes from a realistic and truth-filled assessment of the situation.

> Inappropriate concern is habitual, ongoing and unresolved – not based on truth that comes from the Word of God.

Strategies To Resolve Personal Anxiety

> *Humble yourselves*, therefore, under the mighty hand of God so that at the proper time he may exalt you, **casting all your anxieties on him**, because he cares for you. Be sober-minded; be watchful. Your adversary the devil prowls around like a roaring lion, seeking someone to devour. Resist him, firm in your faith, knowing that the same kinds of suffering are being experienced by your brotherhood throughout the world.
>
> *1 Peter 5:6–9*

Resolving Anxiety Is A Choice

Do not be anxious about tomorrow.

Matthew 6:34

Do not be anxious about anything.

Philippians 4:6

1. Humble Yourselves

- Let go of our own agenda.
- Let go of wrong goals.

Goals and Desires

Any goal that can be blocked by other people or circumstances that you have no right or ability to control is not a goal that God wants you to have. "Downgrade" it to the category of "desire".

---

2. Cast Your Anxiety On To God

Through prayer, determine the following:

- What is God's responsibility?
- What is someone else's responsibility?
- What is your responsibility?

Do what you need to do to fulfil your responsibilities

- Forgiveness
- Repentance
- Making amends

Then leave the rest to God.

> *The Steps To Freedom In Christ* by Neil Anderson (see page 30) contains a very practical way of doing this in its "Anxiety Appendix".

Practise Spiritual Disciplines

Rejoice in the Lord always; again I will say, Rejoice.

Let your reasonableness be known to everyone.

The Lord is at hand; do not be anxious about anything, but in everything by prayer and supplication with thanksgiving

let your requests be made known to God [with thanksgiving].

And the peace of God, which surpasses all understanding, will guard your hearts and your minds in Christ Jesus.

Philippians 4:4–7

1. Rejoice in the Lord always.

2. Let your reasonableness be known to everyone.

3. Be obviously generous and magnanimous.

4. Pray – let your requests be known to God.

5. Give thanks.

6. Persevere until the peace of God guards your heart and mind.

If what we perceive does not reflect the truth, what we feel will not reflect reality.

Choose Your Focus

Finally, brothers, whatever is true, whatever is honourable, whatever is just, whatever is pure, whatever is lovely, whatever is commendable, if there is any excellence, if there is anything worthy of praise, think [and keep on thinking] about these things.

What you have learned and received and heard and seen in me – practise these things, and the God of peace will be with you.

Philippians 4:8–9

- What you have learned – godly discipleship.

- What you have received – godly traditions.

- What you have heard – godly teaching.

- What you have seen – first-hand examples of Christian living.

Recognize That Conflict In Leadership Is Inevitable

Conflict is nothing to be frightened of. It is going to happen from time to time.

The question is simply this: how will you handle it?

Choose To Respond Rather Than React

Reactive – acting out of instinct and reflex.

Responsive – acting out of intention and choice, exercising self-control.

Embrace Pain

God uses pain to develop character in us and in the people we lead.

We need to care for those we lead but we are not responsible for their problems. Just as God refuses to step in and do things that are our responsibility, we need to refuse to step in to "rescue" them or "medicate" them by making them feel better when it would be better for them to persevere and become more mature.

Remember The Sabbath

- Take your holidays.

- Take retreats.

Manage Stress

- Know your vulnerabilities

    What are your particular temptations?

    What is the way of escape?

- Rest, eat, and exercise.

- Control your gadgets.

Wait On The Lord

They who wait for the LORD shall renew their strength;

they shall mount up with wings like eagles;

they shall run and not be weary;

they shall walk and not faint.

Isaiah 40:31

Pause For Thought

We've introduced a number of strategies in this session to help resolve and overcome anxiety in our lives as leaders. Consider ways to implement the strategies in your life.

How do you observe the Sabbath?
Which strategy to overcome anxiety resonated with you most strongly?
What will you do about it?
What has been the biggest insight for you from this session?

Key Themes For Personal Growth As Leaders

We have emphasized the need to work on our *being* as leaders because our doing flows from our being. As we go through *Freed To Lead* you will notice that this boils down to a few key themes:

1. Know who you are in Christ.
2. Ruthlessly close any doors you've opened to the enemy through past sin and don't open any more.
3. Renew your mind to the truth of Gods Word (which is how you will be transformed).
4. Work from a place of rest.

The Leadership Dilemma

Anxiety always hides or disguises itself so we can be completely unaware of our own anxiety and how it is influencing our leadership. Anxiety also undermines the self-control and renewing of the mind we need to help us overcome it.

What was the outcome of your action item(s) from the last session?

How will you apply what you have learned this week?

Pray for one another, focusing especially on anything that seems to be causing anxiety in your group.

You will be encouraged to work through *The Steps To Freedom For Leaders* at the end of this course. But if something in this session has prompted you to want to examine the issue of anxiety in you as a leader more closely, you might like to look at Step 3 (pages 151–156) now.

For further information on the topics covered in this session, see the accompanying book, *Freed To Lead*, by Rod Woods, chapter 10.

SESSION 7:

Overcoming Group Anxiety

PARTICIPANT'S NOTES

What is your strongest personal quality?

Read Psalm 37:21–24.

Pray that your generosity and giving might reflect the generosity and giving of God.

Thank God for the tokens of His generosity in your life.

Read

Read Ephesians 6:10–20 and 2 Timothy 2:24–36.

Read the passages again and mark each word that indicates an adversary to our leadership. What do the marked words suggest about the nature of the battles we face as leaders?

Understand

- Who wrote these passages?
- To whom are these passages written?
- Why were these passages/letters written?

Discern

- What is the purpose of the armour of God?
- What is our ultimate objective in the Ephesians passage (verses 13–14) and in the 2 Timothy passage (verse 26)?
- What is the activity of the devil ("spiritual forces of evil") in the two passages?
- What do you think it means to "pray at all times in the Spirit"?
- What does it look like to be quarrelsome? What is not being quarrelsome according to Paul?
- What is the "snare of the devil"?

Apply

- What does it mean to take a stand and stand firm? How does that relate to leadership?
- Why is it important to keep alert with perseverance?
- We wrestle not against "flesh and blood", but we are to correct "opponents" – clearly meaning people. How do we reconcile the two ideas?
- Why do you think it is so important not to "be quarrelsome", especially as a leader?
- Why does Paul say that God "may perhaps" grant repentance instead of saying that God "will" grant repentance?
- Which comes first: repentance or the knowledge of the truth? Why might this be significant?
- In light of this passage, what might you expect as a leader – both positively and negatively?

Commit

In your leadership, how might you balance the ideas of wrestling not against flesh and blood and correcting your opponents with gentleness?
In light of this passage what might you do as a leader when opposed by people?

Becoming An Anxiety-Resistant Leader

Chronic anxiety has infected the people-systems of society – including churches.

The only way for people-systems to resist and resolve chronic anxiety is to have anxiety-resistant leaders who are totally committed and connected to their people-system.

Remember:

- God gave us a spirit of power and love and self-control (2 Timothy 1:7)
- Put on the whole armour of God (Ephesians 6:11)
- People are not the enemy (Ephesians 6:12)
- Take a stand and then stand firm (Ephesians 6:13–14)

We need to maintain the health of our *being* if we are to become leaders who help people-systems resolve group anxiety.

Five Behaviours Of Anxious People-Systems

1. Reactivity

2. Herding

3. Blame-shifting

4. Quick-fix mentality

5. Leadership abdication.

Reactivity

Reactivity: *a cycle of intense, reflexive reactions between people or groups, "getting stuck" in a negative and sinful way of relating to one another.*

Characteristics Of Reactivity

*   Overly intense emotions

*   Pessimism

*   Violation of legitimate personal boundaries

*   Interrupting, speaking over one another, refusing to listen

*   Overreaction to perceived hurt, insult, or slight

*   Take disagreements too seriously

*   Personal attacks rather than dealing with legitimate issues.

Effects Of Reactivity On People-Systems

- A focus on self-preservation and stability

- Defend and justify reactive behaviour

- A loss of resources

- Destructive and demonized.

Overcoming Reactivity

- Exercise self-control

- Give grace to one another

- Identify and evaluate perceptions

- Respond thoughtfully with gentle firmness – take a stand

- Focus on health – both healthy processes and healthy people

- Move in the opposite spirit

  - Forgiveness not bitterness
  - Calm not anger
  - Appreciation not criticism.

And the Lord's servant must not be quarrelsome but kind to everyone, able to teach, patiently enduring evil, correcting his opponents with gentleness. God may perhaps grant them repentance leading to a knowledge of the truth, and they may come to their senses and escape from the snare of the devil, after being captured by him to do his will.

2 Timothy 2:24–26

Herding

Herding: *a strong pressure for some kind of idealistic cohesion that does not allow people to take responsibility and act maturely.*

Characteristics Of Herding

- A desire to "just get along for the common good"

- Adapting to the least mature, most dependent or dysfunctional member.

Overcoming Herding

- Focus on the mature people in the people-system.

- Emphasize strengths in people and in the people-system.

- Encourage integrity, maturity, and responsibility.

- Be emotionally open and available.

- Take clear, principled stands on issues but remain connected to people.

Blame-Shifting

Blame-shifting: *a focus on forces that are believed to victimize rather than taking personal responsibility for your own being and doing.*

Overcoming Blame-Shifting

- Reframe the issues in relation to the people-system itself.

- Focus on maturity and mature people in the people-system.

- Review perceptions and expectations.

- Describe challenges and respond to those challenges in terms of the healthy aspects of the people-system.

- Encourage people to take appropriate responsibility for themselves by modelling it for them.

Quick-Fix Mentality

Quick-fix mentality: *a low threshold for pain that causes people to seek symptom relief rather than change and maturity.*

Overcoming Quick-Fix Mentality

* Embrace pain and difficulty.

* Encourage, allow and defend time and space for processes to mature.

* Expose idealistic distortions.

* Establish clear and realistic "signposts" to demonstrate progress.

Leadership Abdication

Leadership abdication: *a "failure of nerve" that inclines leaders to neglect the responsibilities of leadership and capitulate to the above-mentioned behaviours.*

Overcoming Leadership Abdication

* Exercise self-control and steadfastness.

* Seek your own maturity and integrity.

* Walk by the Spirit of God.

* Embrace the responsibilities of leadership.

* Accept the consequences of your decisions.

* Commit to persevere in leadership.

* Put a symbolic stake in the ground.

Leading People-Systems Out Of Anxiety

Effective leaders of people-systems:

- take responsibility for themselves so they become anxiety-resistant leaders

- expect relentless resistance, opposition, and sabotage

- submit fully to God

- seek to shape the mindsets of their people-system with faith, hope, and love

- become "lightning rods" – grounded in Jesus and draining away anxiety.

The Leadership Dilemma

Authentic, healthy, connected leaders are the only hope for resolving anxiety in any people-system. But chronically anxious people-systems will always try to eliminate healthy leaders from the system before anxiety is resolved.

> ### Pause For Thought
>
> We really want to emphasize that you *can* overcome anxiety in your people-system. All people-systems will encounter anxiety from time to time – we can't avoid it. But we don't have to be victims.
>
> How have you seen anxiety at work in the various people-systems that you are part of? What has been the impact?
>
> How have you sought to manage and resolve anxiety in the past? How effective has this been?
>
> Think of one way anxiety is manifesting in your people-system. How will you seek to resolve this anxiety based on what you have learned in this session?

What was the outcome of your action item(s) from the last session?

How will you apply what you have learned this week?

Pray for any anxiety present in one another's people-systems. Pray especially that each one would have wisdom for overcoming this anxiety in the people-system.

Reflect on your own leadership experiences using the leadership timeline on page 18:

- Think about some periods when you have experienced personal anxiety. What else was happening around you? How did it affect your leadership?

- . How have you seen group anxiety arise in your leadership context?

You will be encouraged to work through *The Steps To Freedom For Leaders* at the end of this course. But if something in this session has prompted you to want to examine your identity as a leader more closely, you might like to look at Step four (on pages 157–162) now.

> For further information on the topics covered in this session, see the accompanying book, *Freed To Lead,* by Rod Woods, chapter 11.

Building And Keeping Trust

What quality is most important to you in a friend?

Read Psalm 37:25–28.

Thank God for your physical or spiritual children and the promise that they shall become a blessing.

Read

Read 1 Corinthians 4:1–5 and 2 Corinthians 3:1–6.

Read the passages again and note all words containing "commend". Then note all words containing "judg". Finally, note all words containing "sufficie". What stands out to you?

Understand

- Who wrote these passages?
- To whom are the passages written?
- Why were these passages/letters written?

Discern

- What is a "steward"? What is the relationship between being a "steward" and being a "servant"?
- What are the mysteries of God to which Paul is referring?
- What does Paul mean by the words "judge" or "judgment"?

- According to Paul, who is – and is not – the one responsible to "judge"? Why would Paul not even judge himself?
- What does it mean to be "sufficient"? Who has made us sufficient? Does this just apply to our "ministry" or does it apply to our lives generally?
- How does the "letter" kill? How does the Spirit give life?

Apply

- As a leader, what is the gift of God that is in you?
- What is the relationship between "faithfulness" and trust?
- What is the basis of our commendation as leaders?
- What is the possible relationship between our commendation as leaders and our trustworthiness as leaders?
- "The letter kills, but the Spirit gives life." How is this true regarding our leadership?
- In light of this passage, what might you expect as a leader – both positively and negatively?

Commit

- How will this passage affect your tendency to judge yourself and your leadership (as well as the leadership of others)?

Trust

This is how one should regard us, as servants of Christ and stewards of the mysteries of God. Moreover, it is required of stewards that they be found trustworthy.

1 Corinthians 4:1–2

Pause For Thought

In our hearts we know that trust is important, but perhaps we do not appreciate how important trust really is to our effectiveness as leaders as well as to the health of our people-systems.

Who is the person you most trust in your life? Why?

Do you consider yourself worthy of trust as a leader? Why or why not?

How would you define "trust"?

Indicators Of A Low Trust People-System

Atmosphere Of Suspicion

- Manipulated or distorted facts
- Spinning the truth
- Withholding information
- Blaming, criticism, accusation
- Secrets and secret meetings.

Atmosphere Of Anxiety

- Unwillingness to take risks
- Mistakes covered up
- Overpromising and underdelivering.

Atmosphere Of Tension And Friction

- Getting personal credit is important
- Open resistance to new ideas and change
- Unrealistic expectations.

Indicators Of A High Trust People-System

Atmosphere Of Openness

- Information is shared openly
- Mistakes are tolerated and encouraged
- Authenticity and vulnerability are demonstrated
- Accountability.

Atmosphere Of Honour

- A focus on others instead of self
- Sharing credit
- Honesty
- Loyalty to those not present
- Collaboration and co-operation.

Atmosphere Of Creativity

- Energy and vitality
- Reduced anxiety
- Enhanced teamwork
- Increased innovation and better execution
- Improved communication.

The Atmosphere Of Trust That God Creates

One of the most significant things you can do as a leader is make sure you yourself have a deep understanding of the grace of God. Then simply come to your people the same way God comes to you.

God:

1. Gives us a huge commission and the means to fulfil it
2. Trusts us to do what He has called us to do
3. Gives us freedom to fail
4. Disciplines us in love
5. Is always available
6. Shows unswerving loyalty even when we are disloyal
7. Is slow to anger and abounding in steadfast love. (Psalm 103:8)

Building Trust

All trust flows from two dynamics: being and doing.

Being (Character)	**Doing** (Competence)
Integrity	Abilities
Motive	Skills
Intent	Tangible track record

Trust: *to place your confidence in the being and doing of another.*

The Trust Equation

If people feel your character (being) is right and you are competent (doing), they will trust you.

$$QB + QD = C$$

Quality of *Being* + Quality of *Doing* = Amount of *Confidence*

The Apostle Paul On Building Trust

Are we beginning to commend ourselves again? Or do we need, as some do, letters of recommendation to you, or from you? You yourselves are our letter of recommendation, written on our hearts, to be known and read by all. And you show that you are a letter from Christ delivered by us, written not with ink but with the Spirit of the living God, not on tablets of stone but on tablets of human hearts.

2 Corinthians 3:1–3

Such is the confidence that we have through Christ towards God. Not that we are sufficient in ourselves to claim anything as coming from us, but our sufficiency is from God, who has made us competent to be ministers of a new covenant, not of the letter but of the Spirit. For the letter kills, but the Spirit gives life.

2 Corinthians 3:4–5

What we are is known to God, and I hope it is known also to your conscience. We are not commending ourselves to you again but giving you cause to boast about us, so that you may be able to answer those who boast about outward appearance and not about what is in the heart.

2 Corinthians 5:11–12

Trust-Building Behaviours Of Being (Character)

Speak the truth in love

Rather, speaking the truth in love, we are to grow up in every way into him who is the head, into Christ, from whom the whole body, joined and held together by every joint with which it is equipped, when each part is working properly, makes the body grow so that it builds itself up in love.

Ephesians 4:15–16

Show respect and honour

Pay to all what is owed to them: taxes to whom taxes are owed, revenue to whom revenue is owed, respect to whom respect is owed, honour to whom honour is owed.

Romans 13:7

Model transparency

But above all, my brothers, do not swear, either by heaven or by earth or by any other oath, but let your "yes" be yes and your "no" be no, so that you may not fall under condemnation.

James 5:12

Right wrongs

So if you are offering your gift at the altar and there remember that your brother has something against you, leave your gift there before the altar and go. First be reconciled to your brother, and then come and offer your gift. Come to terms quickly with your accuser while you are going with him to court, lest your accuser hand you over to the judge, and the judge to the guard, and you be put in prison.

Matthew 5:23–25

Show loyalty

Many a man proclaims his own steadfast love, but a faithful man who can find?

Proverbs 20:6

Pay attention to others

Let each of you look not only to his own interests, but also to the interests of others.

Philippians 2:4

Exercise self-control

It is not good to eat much honey, nor is it glorious to seek one's own glory. A man without self-control is like a city broken into and left without walls.

Proverbs 25:27–28

Express gratitude

Let there be no filthiness nor foolish talk nor crude joking, which are out of place, but instead let there be thanksgiving.

Ephesians 5:4

Give grace

Be kind to one another, tender-hearted, forgiving one another, as God in Christ forgave you.

Ephesians 4:32

Trust-Building Behaviours Of Doing (Competence)

Deliver results – don't make excuses

Keep your conduct among the Gentiles honourable, so that when they speak against you as evildoers, they may see your good deeds and glorify God on the day of visitation.

1 Peter 2:12

Get better – continually improve on what you do

Give instruction to a wise man, and he will be still wiser; teach a righteous man, and he will increase in learning.

Proverbs 9:9

Confront reality

And Samuel came to Saul, and Saul said to him, "Blessed be you to the LORD. I have performed the commandment of the LORD." And Samuel said, "What then is this bleating of the sheep in my ears and the lowing of the oxen that I hear?" Saul said, "They have brought them from the Amalekites, for the people spared the best of the sheep and of the oxen to sacrifice to the LORD your God, and the rest we have devoted to destruction."

1 Samuel 15:13–15

Clarify expectations

So I thought it necessary to urge the brothers to go on ahead to you and arrange in advance for the gift you have promised, so that it may be ready as a willing gift, not as an exaction. The point is this: whoever sows sparingly will also reap sparingly, and whoever sows bountifully will also reap bountifully. Each one must give as he has decided in his heart, not reluctantly or under compulsion, for God loves a cheerful giver.

2 Corinthians 9:5–7

Practise accountability

So then each of us will give an account of himself to God.

Romans 14:12

Listen actively

Know this, my beloved brothers: let every person be quick to hear, slow to speak, slow to anger; for the anger of man does not produce the righteousness of God.

James 1:19–20

Keep commitments

O LORD, who shall sojourn in your tent? Who shall dwell on your holy hill? ... [he] who swears to his own hurt and does not change;

Psalm 15:1 and 4b

Extend trust to others

And some of the men of Benjamin and Judah came to the stronghold to David. David went out to meet them and said to them, "If you have come to me in friendship to help me, my heart will be joined to you; but if to betray me to my adversaries, although there is no wrong in my hands, then may the God of our fathers see and rebuke you." Then the Spirit clothed Amasai, chief of the thirty, and he said, "We are yours, O David, and with you, O son of Jesse! Peace, peace to you, and peace to your helpers! For your God helps you." Then David received them and made them officers of his troops.

1 Chronicles 12:16–18

Meet the needs of followers

Now in these days when the disciples were increasing in number, a complaint by the Hellenists arose against the Hebrews because their widows were being neglected in the daily distribution. And the twelve summoned the full number of the disciples and said, "It is not right that we should give up preaching the word of God to serve tables. Therefore, brothers, pick out from among you seven men of good repute, full of the Spirit and of wisdom, whom we will appoint to this duty. But we will devote ourselves to prayer and to the ministry of the word." And what they said pleased the whole gathering, and they chose Stephen, a man full of faith and of the Holy Spirit, and Philip, and Prochorus, and Nicanor, and Timon, and Parmenas, and Nicolaus, a proselyte of Antioch. These they set before the apostles, and they prayed and laid their hands on them.

Acts 6:1–6

Losing And Regaining Trust

Trust takes time to build but can be lost in an instant.

The quickest way to destroy trust is for your behaviour to cause people to doubt your being – your integrity, your goodwill. That will happen if you violate a trust-building behaviour of being.

The quickest way to increase trust is through your doing – your actions, your abilities, your competence.

To rebuild trust you must:

- Stop violating trust-building behaviours of being
- Intentionally practise trust-building behaviours of doing.

The Leadership Dilemma

People-systems can't function without trust. But they are increasingly prone to anxiety which degrades trust. Increasingly society itself is a low-trust environment with people actively trying to destroy trust in leaders. The end result is that there is a corrosive pessimism towards leaders and people-systems.

Pause For Thought

Hopefully this session has helped you understand some ways we can increase trust in ourselves as leaders.

How have you experienced the negative effects of the lack of trust in a person or system?

How have you experienced the benefits of trust?

Based on what you have learned in this session, what one or two things could you do to improve your competence and credibility as a leader so that people might trust you more?

What was the outcome of your action item(s) from the last session?

How will you apply what you have learned this week?

Pray for one another, focusing on trust-building behaviours that each person would like to adopt or improve in their leadership.

For further information on the topics covered in this session, see the accompanying book, *Freed To Lead,* by Rod Woods, chapter 13.

SESSION 9:

Overcoming Personal Pitfalls

PARTICIPANT'S NOTES

WELCOME

Why did you choose your profession or leadership position?

WORSHIP

Read Psalm 37:29–31.

Surrender yourselves to God afresh and ask God to put His will in your heart.

WORD

Read

Read 1 Corinthians 10:6–13.

What are the Old Testament stories to which Paul is referring?

Understand

- Who wrote this passage?
- To whom is this passage written?
- Why was this passage/letter written?

Discern

- What does it mean to "desire evil"? What is the relationship between this and "temptation"?
- What does it mean to put Christ to the test?
- Why does Paul give the warning of verse 12? What does it mean?
- What are the promises in verse 13?

Apply

- What are some common "idols" leaders might have?
- When are we most likely to "grumble" as leaders? What effect does this have on our leadership?
- How do you feel about the fact that you will not face an uncommon temptation (verse 13)?
- Why does Paul suggest that we have to "endure" temptation (verse 13)?
- What is the "way of escape"? When is it easiest to escape temptation?

Commit

- What temptations have you been able to resist or overcome as a leader? How have you seen God's faithfulness in this?
- What "instruction" (verse 11) from this passage will you apply to your leadership?

Pause For Thought

Remember: having struggles and difficulties as a leader does not mean you are not a good leader.

What are the greatest challenges you face personally as a leader?
What are the greatest temptations you face personally as a leader?

Types Of Personal Leadership Pitfall

Pitfalls: *hidden or unexpected dangers or difficulties.*

1. Temptation

2. Self-centredness

3. Emotional

4. Communication

5. Exhaustion.

Temptation Pitfalls

Temptations pitfalls: *strong temptations to find significance, security, and acceptance outside of God.*

Money – including all the financial and material resources God has provided

- Poor personal and organisational money management – debt, bill paying, giving.
- Attitudes about money – greed, covetousness, envy.

Sex

- Wrong ways of thinking – fantasy, daydreaming, lust.
- Wrong actions – pornography, immorality, adultery.
- Wrong situations –"one to one" with no code of practice.

Power

- Desire for control, position or titles, respect.
- Manipulation and dominance.

Avoiding Temptation Pitfalls

- Lead from your identity in Christ – you are significant, secure, and accepted.
- Guard your heart and mind.
- Take the way of escape.
  1 Corinthians 10:13 promises a way of escape from *every* temptation. Where is it? Right at the start of the process, when the tempting thought first comes into your mind.

Paul says in Romans 6 that the power of sin is broken in your life if you are a Christian. That is the truth whether it *feels* true or not.

Self-Centredness Pitfalls

Self-centredness pitfalls: *thinking of leadership from a self-centred perspective.*

Messiah – thinking that you are the saviour of your system or situation

- Arrogance
- Pride
- Selfish ambition
- Manipulation.

A messiah pitfall arises from trying to find significance in leadership rather than in Jesus.

Martyr – thinking that your system requires your suffering or sacrifice to achieve good outcomes

- Control
- Manipulation through shame or guilt
- Avoidance.

A martyr pitfall arises from trying to find acceptance in leadership rather than in Jesus.

Hermit – feeling overwhelmed by stress, conflict, problems or responsibilities

- Retreat
- Narrow focus
- Ignore people
- Deny reality
- Passivity and acquiescence
- Cowardice – a failure of nerve.

A hermit pitfall arises from trying to find security in leadership rather than in Jesus.

Emotional Pitfalls

Emotional pitfalls: *following or being controlled by strong, negative emotions.*

Bitterness – failing to forgive others

- Physical problems such as ulcers
- Disrupted and destroyed relationships
- Malice
- Hatred.

Anger – having a blocked goal

- Resentment
- Frustration
- Impatience
- Irritation
- Rage.

Defensiveness – seeking to protect and justify yourself, taking offence

- Oversensitive
- Thin-skinned
- Prickly
- Overly emotional.

Christian leaders never need to defend themselves. If you are wrong, you don't have a defence. If you are right, you don't need a defence because God Himself will defend you.

Communication Pitfalls

Communication pitfalls: *failing to recognize common aspects of communication which can be mistaken as attack or rebellion.*

- Communication engages emotions and is not just an intellectual process
- Be aware of the effects of distance
- Pursuit behaviours such as criticizing and rescuing often indicate a person's desire to engage in communication yet they tend to turn the other person away.

Avoiding Communication Pitfalls

- Engage humour in communication
- Use "close" communication – face-to-face is best – for difficult subjects
- Allow yourself to be "caught" by those engaging in pursuit behaviours:
    - Stop what you are doing and be emotionally open
    - Listen actively
    - Do not assume rebellion or personal attack.

Exhaustion Pitfalls

Exhaustion pitfalls: *failing to rest and recharge our spiritual, emotional, and relational "batteries".*

Blowout – falling into serious sin because of physical, emotional, mental, and spiritual exhaustion

- Sexual Immorality
- "Too much" syndrome
- Sudden sickness or major health issues.

Bankruptcy – the point at which we run out of spiritual, mental, and emotional reserves and insights

- Loss of creativity
- Loss of vitality
- "Recycling" of insights, messages and teachings.

Burnout – a long-term physical, emotional, mental, and spiritual exhaustion

- Overwhelmed
- Helpless
- Hopeless
- Cynical
- Resentful.

Avoiding Exhaustion Pitfalls

"Abide in me, and I in you. As the branch cannot bear fruit by itself, unless it abides in the vine, neither can you, unless you abide in me."

John 15:4

- We get tired because we want to bear fruit.
- Jesus wants us to bear fruit even more than we do ourselves.
- His command, however, was not to bear fruit but to abide in Him.
- We will bear fruit only if we are connected to Jesus, working from a place of internal rest.

*So then, there remains a Sabbath rest for the people of God, for whoever has entered God's rest has also rested from his works as God did from his. Let us therefore **strive** to enter that rest, so that no one may fall by the same sort of disobedience.*

Hebrews 4:9–11

- Prioritize prayer and Bible reading.
- Take time out to seek God and His will for your life.
- Rest.

Avoiding Personal Pitfalls

- Use *The Steps To Freedom In Christ* regularly (see page 30).
- Practise accountability, vulnerability, honesty, humility.
- Practise lifelong learning – take retreats, read books, listen to lectures.
- Remind yourself how damaging pitfalls are personally and to your leadership.

Put on the Lord Jesus Christ, and make no provision for the flesh, to gratify its desires.

Romans 13:14

Pause For Thought

This pause for thought encourages you to get a little vulnerable with one another.

Which "pit" have you fallen into already?
What steps will you take to get out of it?
Which "pit" are you closest to falling into at this moment?
What steps will you take to avoid falling in?

The Leadership Dilemma

We have everything we need in Christ to avoid these pitfalls, but even so, if we are not very careful, we will tend to keep falling into them.

REMINDER! Key Themes For Personal Growth As Leaders

1. Know who you are in Christ.
2. Ruthlessly close any doors you've opened to the enemy through past sin and don't open any more.
3. Renew your mind to the truth of God's Word (which is how you will be transformed).
4. Work from a place of rest.

What was the outcome of your action item(s) from the last session?

How will you apply what you have learned this week?

Pray for one another in the personal pitfalls that you might be facing.

You will be encouraged to work through *The Steps To Freedom For Leaders* at the end of this course. But if something in this session has prompted you to want to examine the area of pitfalls in your personal life you might like to look at Steps 5 and 6 (pages 163–179) now.

For further information on the topics covered in this session, see the accompanying book, *Freed To Lead*, by Rod Woods, chapters 12 and 14.

Words From An Older Leader To A Younger Leader

You then, my child, be strengthened by the grace that is in Christ Jesus, and what you have heard from me in the presence of many witnesses entrust to faithful men who will be able to teach others also. Share in suffering as a good soldier of Christ Jesus. No soldier gets entangled in civilian pursuits, since his aim is to please the one who enlisted him. An athlete is not crowned unless he competes according to the rules. It is the hard-working farmer who ought to have the first share of the crops. Think over what I say, for the Lord will give you understanding in everything.

2 Timothy 2:1–7

SESSION 10:

Overcoming Group Pitfalls

PARTICIPANT'S NOTES

What famous person would you like to have a meal with? And what is the first question you'd want to ask that person?

Read Psalm 37:32–36.

Surrender any difficult situations or relationships you have to God, asking for His deliverance.

Thank God that He will not abandon you, that He will be your defender.

WORD

Read

Read Corinthians 2:1–11.

Read the passage again. Note all the words to do with "pain". What strikes you about the results?

Understand

- Who wrote this passage?
- To whom is this passage written?
- Why was this passage/letter written?

Discern

- According to Paul, who or what has caused pain?
- What is the connection between pain and love in verse 4?
- What are the godly Christian responses to pain and those who cause us pain in this passage?

Apply

- What role does "pain" play in leadership?
- How and when might leaders justly cause pain in others?
- How might Satan outwit us if we do not respond to pain appropriately?
- What are some of the "designs" or "schemes" of Satan that might emerge in painful situations?
- According to this passage, what are some possible consequences of sinful behaviour to a people-system?
- Why is forgiveness so important to Paul in this passage?
- In light of this passage, what might you expect as a leader – both positively and negatively?

Commit

In your leadership, when have you experienced pain? When might you have caused pain? How did you respond? How might you respond differently now?

How have you seen Satan's schemes at work in the painful situations you've faced? What strategies might you employ to overcome those schemes?

Group Pitfalls

Group pitfalls: *a set of predictable (but not inevitable) reactions within your people-system in response to **effective** leadership.*

- Effective leadership will *always* trigger a number of reactions.
- These reactions indicate that our leadership is effective!
- It's not the reaction itself that is the pitfall but our potential wrong response to it.

Dilemmas Not Problems

Problems – issues that can be solved and resolved.

Dilemmas – issues that by their nature cannot be solved, only managed.

Group pitfalls are *dilemmas* and require time and effort to work through.

Four Common Group Pitfalls

1. Selfishness
2. Sabotage
3. Strife
4. Suffering.

Selfishness

Selfishness: *an inappropriate focus on self.*

Symptoms of selfishness:

- Self-centred
- Self-seeking
- Self-referential
- Immaturity – unwillingness or inability to take responsibility for one's mind, will and emotions. Often mistaken for rebellion.

To help your people-system avoid the pitfall of selfishness:

- Model healthy self-giving
- Promote maturity by being mature – take responsibility
- Focus on healthy and mature people in the system without giving in to selfishness.

Sabotage

Sabotage: *seeking to destroy, damage, obstruct, or hinder leaders or change.*

Sources of sabotage:

- Personal or political advantage
- Changing relationships and jealousy
- Fleshly attitudes
- Pride
- Demonically inspired.

Common ways that sabotage presents itself:

- Spreading discontent
- Magnifying the potential loss of doing something
- Misrepresenting a leader or a decision
- Passive aggressive behaviour
- Changing your mind after the group has made a decision
- Putting in extra conditions on an agreement late in negotiations or even after negotiations have been completed
- Agreeing publicly while undermining something privately
- Spreading gossip and rumours
- Bullying and intimidation.

To help your people-system avoid the pitfall of sabotage:

- Respond calmly, peacefully, and intentionally
- Focus on building healthy people and healthy processes.

Strife

Strife: *friction and conflict in the people-system; problems within interpersonal relationships.*

Symptoms of strife:

- Reactivity
- Arguments
- Conflicts of will
- Criticism
- Personal attacks.

Ineffective actions when facing strife:

- Explaining or justifying your position
- Defending yourself
- Withdrawing from the conflict and refusing to engage
- Blaming
- Placating or appeasing
- Bargaining.

To help your people-system avoid the pitfall of strife:

- Ensure that you are grounded in Jesus Christ
- Encourage people to work through strife with love, mercy, and grace
- Model appropriate responses to strife.

Suffering

Suffering: *experiencing something that you perceive to be negative or unpleasant.*

Your willingness and ability to embrace suffering will determine the willingness and ability of the people-system you lead to embrace suffering.

Overcoming Group Pitfalls

- Lead from your identity
- Gain fresh perspective
- Welcome conflict as normal and healthy for growth
- Embrace suffering
- Resist idealistic distortions and expectations.

Pause For Thought

Most people tend to assume that we face group pitfalls because we're not leading well rather than because of *effective* leadership.

Does it surprise you that group pitfalls are the result of healthy leadership? Why or why not?

Which group pitfalls have you seen or experienced personally? What has been the effect on the people-system?

Have you ever sabotaged something? What would have been a healthier response?

Leadership Delusions

Delusion: *a false belief or impression we maintain even when it is contradicted by reality.*

Four Leadership Delusions

1. Expertise
2. Empathy
3. Togetherness
4. Position.

The Delusion Of Expertise

The delusion of expertise: *a false belief that maintains that the right knowledge or technique will make us effective leaders.*

The Delusion Of Empathy

The delusion of empathy: *a false belief that maintains that understanding and sensitivity alone will make us effective leaders. It also maintains that we can overcome inappropriate, unhealthy or destructive behaviour with reason, fairness, and sensitivity.*

The Delusion Of Togetherness

The delusion of togetherness: *a false belief that promoting or maintaining consensus will make us effective leaders.*

Togetherness is sometimes mistaken for unity.

The Delusion Of Position

The delusion of position: *a false belief that position, title, or power will make us effective leaders.*

Dispelling Delusions

- Expose the faulty thinking associated with these delusions.
- Lead from your identity in Christ.
- Hold everything loosely – except Jesus.

Pause For Thought

When thinking about leadership delusions, it's easy for us to get caught up in an either/or mentality. Either things like expertise and empathy are good, or they are bad. However, there's nothing wrong with expertise, empathy, a little togetherness, or having a position of leadership. The delusion is that any of these things in and of themselves will help us lead more effectively. In other words, these are not leadership strategies.

Which delusion have you succumbed to in the past?

What steps will you take to dispel that delusion?

How have you seen others get wrapped up in one or more of the delusions?

The Leadership Dilemma

We call these dilemmas "group pitfalls", but our *being* and *doing* as leaders will determine more than anything else whether our people-systems get stuck in them.

> *For this reason I remind you to fan into flame the gift of God, which is in you through the laying on of my hands, for God gave us a spirit not of fear [or cowardice] but of power and love and self-control.*
>
> 2 Timothy 1:6–7

What was the outcome of your action item(s) from the last session?

How will you apply what you have learned this week?

Pray for one another to have the courage to respond to any group pitfalls in healthy, responsible ways.

Bless one another in your leadership roles and responsibilities.

For further information on the topics covered in this session, see the accompanying book, *Freed To Lead*, by Rod Woods, chapters 15 and 16.

Transforming Leadership

PARTICIPANT'S NOTES

These notes accompany the introduction to Step Seven of *The Steps To Freedom For Leaders*.

> *Now I rejoice in my sufferings for your sake, and in my flesh I am filling up what is lacking in Christ's afflictions for the sake of his body, that is, the church, of which I became a minister according to the stewardship from God that was given to me for you, to make the word of God fully known, the mystery hidden for ages and generations but now revealed to his saints. To them God chose to make known how great among the Gentiles are the riches of the glory of this mystery, which is Christ in you, the hope of glory. Him we proclaim, warning everyone and teaching everyone with all wisdom, that we may present everyone mature in Christ. For this I toil, struggling with all his energy that he powerfully works within me.*
> *Colossians 1:24-29*

WATCH ➡

Because Christ Is In Us

We May Become Authentically Ourselves As Leaders

We Have Real Hope
- Our leadership will bring glory to God.
- Our leadership will change lives.
- Our leadership will show Jesus Christ to the world.

We Can Develop Abilities To Boost Our Growth And Effectiveness

1. Know ourselves

We need to give up trying to be someone or something other than who we are.

2. Control ourselves

Self-control is the only biblical form of control.

3. Communicate ourselves

Vulnerability indicates strength: only a strong person will have the courage and ability to become vulnerable.

We Can Transform Our Leadership Through:

1. **Love** – a zealous, self-giving commitment to others for their benefit.

2. **Faith** – choosing to trust and act, often beyond our natural abilities, based on true knowledge of God and His ways. It is founded in relationship through Jesus Christ in the power of the Holy Spirit.

3. **Embracing the cross:**
   - Offering up our reputation and good name
   - Allowing people to revile us and say all manner of evil against us falsely
   - Being excluded and rejected
   - Laying down our "weapons"
   - Accepting the pain of leadership.

4. **Perseverance and endurance**
   - Perseverance – steadfastness in doing something despite difficulty or delay
   - Endurance – bearing up under something that is difficult or unpleasant without giving way.

"The man who can drive himself further once the effort gets painful is the man who will win." (Roger Bannister)

5. **Perspective** – our reference point from which we view our circumstances.

For further information on the topics covered in this session, see the accompanying book, *Freed To Lead*, by Rod Woods, chapter 17.

The Steps To Freedom For Leaders

Introduction

The Steps To Freedom In Christ by Neil T. Anderson is a resource used around the world to help Christians resolve personal and spiritual issues. Based on his books *Victory Over The Darkness* and *The Bondage Breaker*, and founded on the teaching in the Freedom In Christ Discipleship Course, the "Steps" have become an essential discipleship tool for many churches around the world. Churches use the Steps in a variety of ways: in corporate settings, where people pray through the Steps personally as part of a large-group process; in personal settings, where people pray through the Steps with an encourager and a prayer partner; and in individual settings, where people pray through the Steps or use portions of the Steps as part of their personal discipleship. For many churches the Steps are a fundamental part of their ministry, serving as a doorway into church membership or ministry.

The Steps To Freedom For Leaders is a resource focused on the personal and spiritual issues common to people in leadership, be it leadership in the marketplace, leadership in the church, or leadership in the home and community. This resource will enable you to identify and resolve personal and spiritual issues that can weaken, undermine, or even destroy your leadership. In some cases, these issues have become so entwined with our understanding of leadership that we do not even realize that what we are doing is actually preventing us from being the leaders God desires.

How To Use The Leadership Steps

You may use *The Steps To Freedom For Leaders* in the same ways as you can use the original Steps To Freedom: group settings; personal settings; and individual settings. As with the original Steps, we most strongly recommend using the Leadership Steps in a personal setting with an encourager and a prayer partner. Alternatively, two leaders praying through *The Steps To Freedom For Leaders* together would prove very effective.

However you choose to work through the Leadership Steps, it is essential to give yourself time for reflection as you go through the prayer process. Make notes about the various things you sense that God is showing you about yourself and your leadership. Ideas and strategies may come to your mind regarding your present leadership context. Write these ideas down immediately so that they do not distract you from listening to God for how He is calling you to change and grow as a leader.

In order to receive the maximum benefit from using *The Steps To Freedom For Leaders*, we recommend the following:

- Participating in the Freedom In Christ Discipleship Course, reading the four accompanying *Discipleship Series* books by Steve Goss or reading *Victory Over The Darkness* and *The Bondage Breaker* by Neil T. Anderson
- Engaging in *The Steps To Freedom In Christ* in a personal setting
- Familiarity with the "Truth About My Father God" exercise in Step Two of *The Steps To Freedom In Christ*
- Familiarity with the "Stronghold-Busting" exercise taught in the Freedom In Christ Discipleship Course
- Integrating the discipleship truths from the above fully into your life in an ongoing way
- Participating in the *Freed To Lead* course or reading the *Freed To Lead* book by Rod Woods.

In addition to the above, we would also recommend *The Grace Course* from Freedom In Christ Ministries, a course designed to help people overcome common issues regarding grace and legalism. Such legalism is one of the most destructive forces in the life of a leader – just consider the Pharisees in Jesus' day.

Discipleship For Leaders

As with the general Steps, *The Steps To Freedom For Leaders* provide a number of discipleship resources that may be used outside the overall Leadership Steps process to keep your leadership free in Christ and healthy. For example, we would encourage the use of Step 2 (Forgiveness) on a regular basis to ensure that you are forgiving those who wound you in your leadership context. By so doing, you will overcome the unforgiveness and bitterness issues that have destroyed or seriously damaged many leaders. You could use Step 3 (Anxiety and Reactivity) to help your team work together more smoothly and overcome the anxiety in the face of change that often undermines a team's creativity.

As with *The Steps to Freedom In Christ,* we encourage you to use *The Steps To Freedom for Leaders* annually as scheduled maintenance for your leadership.

However you may use *The Steps To Freedom For Leaders,* we pray that God will richly bless your leadership wherever He has called you. We pray that your exercise of leadership will result in praise and glory to our Lord and Saviour, Jesus Christ.

Opening Prayer And Declaration

Before you begin with the opening prayer and declaration, spend a few minutes reflecting on the following questions (or discussing them with your encourager if you are doing this in a personal setting):

- Who is the most influential leader in your life?
- What qualities do you admire most in a leader?
- What qualities most annoy you in a leader?
- What do you remember most about the leadership qualities of your parents?
- Do you see yourself as a leader? Why or why not?
- Do you see yourself as a good leader? Why or why not?
- What talents, skills, knowledge, and spiritual gifts do you have that you use regularly in your leadership?
- What qualities of Jesus' leadership would you like to see grow in your own leadership?
- How would you like to be remembered as a leader ten years from now?
- What is the greatest legacy that you would like to leave as a leader?

If you have a journal, you may want to make notes about your responses to these questions for review each time you work through *The Steps to Freedom For Leaders.*

Opening Prayer

Dear Heavenly Father, I acknowledge You as the one true living God, existing as the Father, Son and Holy Spirit, and the only Lord of my life. I choose to surrender myself fully to You, so that I may become the leader You have created me to be. I give thanks to You that you have reconciled me to Yourself by grace through faith in Your Son, Jesus Christ. I pray that You, the God of our Lord Jesus Christ, the Father of glory, may give me the Spirit of wisdom and of revelation in the knowledge of Jesus. I pray that I may have the eyes of my heart enlightened, so that I may know what is the hope to which You have called me and what are the riches of Your glorious inheritance in the saints. I pray that I may know the immeasurable greatness of Your power towards us who believe, according to the working of Your great might that You worked in Christ when You raised Him from the dead and seated Him at Your right hand in the heavenly places (Ephesians 1:16-20). I want to know and choose to do Your will in the leadership to which You have called me. To that end, I welcome Your Holy Spirit and Your people to lead me in this process. I choose to co-operate with You fully to the glory of my Lord and Saviour, Jesus Christ. Amen.

Declaration

In the name of Jesus Christ, as one sealed by the Spirit of God, I declare that I submit fully to God and resist the devil (James 4:7). I command Satan and all evil spirits to release me and have no influence over me so that I can know and do God's will. I exalt the living Lord Jesus Christ as the One who died on the cross and rose bodily from the dead, who is now seated far above all rule and authority and power and dominion, and above every name that is named, not only in this age but also in the one to come. This Jesus has all things under His feet and is the head over all things for the benefit of the Church, which is His body, the fullness of Him who fills all in all, and of which I am part (Ephesians 1:21-23). I declare that I, _____(name), belong to Christ and the evil one cannot touch me (1 John 5:18). I declare that I surrender myself fully – my hopes, dreams and leadership – to God the Father, through Jesus Christ the Son, and in the power of the Holy Spirit. Amen.

Step One: Embracing Our Identity In Christ, Not Leadership

The purpose of this Step is to help discern ways in which you have sought identity, significance, security, or acceptance in leadership roles, positions and titles rather than in Jesus Christ.

To the degree that we try to find our sense of significance, security, acceptance, or identity in our leadership, our leadership is likely to be distorted or dysfunctional. To the degree that we find all these things in Jesus, we will discover true freedom to lead as the people God has created us to be.

You are not free to lead if you are finding your identity in your role as a leader, or if you are basing your acceptance on the approval of others, hoping for job security, or finding your significance in what you do as a leader.

If you could no longer function as a leader or serve in your current leadership capacity, would you still be the same person, having the same sense of acceptance, security, and significance?

Use Part 1 below to help you determine the degree to which you have found your significance, security, acceptance, or identity in leadership.

Part 1 – Discerning Wrongful Identity In Leadership

Dear Heavenly Father,

I thank You that by Your grace through faith in Your Son Jesus Christ I have become your chosen child, holy and precious to You. I thank you that in Christ I know that I am significant, secure, and accepted. However, I confess that I have not always chosen to believe that my identity was fully in Christ. I have sought significance, security, and acceptance through my leadership. I ask that Your Holy Spirit reveal to my mind all the ways that I have sinned against You in this regard, so that I might repent. In Jesus' name, I pray. Amen.

Consider the following four lists. Rate each statement in them on a scale of 1 to 5, with 1 being something that is not at all true for you and 5 being something that is very true for you.

Write the total at the base of each section.

Discerning whether we have sought our identity in leadership:

Identity is more than a label. It speaks to the essence of who we are and why we are here. When we begin our journey on earth, the world seems to revolve around us. Inevitably flesh patterns develop over time until we discover who we are in Christ and learn to centre our life around Christ. Such flesh patterns will hinder our ability to lead.

- _ I have trouble imagining my life without my leadership responsibilities.
- _ I often feel that my "world" revolves around my leadership role.
- _ I often take my electronic gadgets on holiday with me so that I can keep up with my leadership responsibilities.
- _ I often struggle to stop thinking about my work/leadership role, even when I have a day off or a holiday.
- _ All my hobbies and leisure activities tend to relate to my leadership role.
- _ I feel that my leadership role is the most significant and meaningful part of my life.
- _ My spouse, children, or friends often complain that I spend too much time in my leadership role (or at work).
- _ I feel proud to have attained the leadership position I have
- _ I deeply relish all the benefits of the leadership position I have attained and would find it very difficult to lose them.
- _ When I am talking with people, the first thing I tend to talk about is something to do with my leadership role or responsibilities.
- _ **Total**

Discerning whether we have sought our significance in leadership:

What is forgotten in time is of little significance. What is remembered for eternity has the greatest significance. Believing we are insignificant or that our ministries are insignificant will cripple our leadership as will try to find our significance in leadership roles.

- I feel that if I did not do the work myself then everything would fall apart.
- My leadership role or position gives me a sense that I have a place in this world.
- I am a very important part of my organization, perhaps the key to its success.
- I focus a lot on the number of people who attend my event, or the publicity it receives.
- How much money I make shows the value of my leadership. (Or: How much money I could be making if I were in another field shows the value of my leadership.)
- I enjoy telling people the number of emails that I receive each day, the number of people I supervise, or how important my responsibilities are.
- I feel hurt or upset when I do not get the credit that I deserve.
- I pay much attention to – or draw others' attention to – the number of titles and degrees I have.
- I find it difficult to rest because people really need my help or input.
- My leadership role helps me feel good about myself.
- **Total**

Discerning whether we have sought our security in leadership:

Security relates to eternal rather than temporal matters, which we have no right or ability to control. Insecure leaders will try to manipulate people and events that they believe will offer them some sense of security.

- I'm not sure what I would do in my life if I could not continue in my current leadership role or position.
- I often feel that I must remain in control of the situation.
- When people criticize me, I often find myself getting very defensive.
- All my friends and social circles seem to revolve around my leadership role.
- If someone were to wrong me at work or in my leadership capacity, I would quickly seek redress through appropriate channels.
- As a leader, it is important for me to remain in charge of situations.

- I often find myself reminding people how busy I am.
- I feel competitive or jealous when others seem to do well at the same things I do.
- I feel threatened when I am with others who seem to be more successful than I am.
- I spend a lot of time thinking about how much I am paid for my leadership role.
- **Total**

Discerning whether we have sought our acceptance in leadership:

Acceptance by God is more than being tolerated. It means that we are fully forgiven, adopted as a child of God, made a new creation in Christ, and welcomed as a valuable member into the family of God. Knowing this is essential for leaders, who are likely to receive more criticism and rejection than followers.

- I struggle to say "no" to new responsibilities.
- I find it difficult to share my personal struggles with others in my leadership sphere or with the people I lead.
- As a leader, I feel it is very important for me to be liked by those around me.
- I conceal my thoughts and feelings because if others see the "real me" they would not want me or allow me to be a leader.
- I really want people to address me by my title or position.
- I have a difficult time admitting when I make a mistake, especially regarding my leadership.
- I will often do something others want me to even when I know that it might not be for the best.
- I find myself spending much of my time as a leader simply reacting to the needs and crises of others.
- I often neglect to take a day off because people urgently need me.
- I find it very difficult when people criticize or reject me.
- **Total**

Look at your totals in each of the four areas above and take some time to assess before God how significant an issue each area is for you.

We would suggest that a total of 40–50 in an area indicates that this area is definitely an issue for you; 30–40 indicates it is probably an issue for you; 20–30 indicates it may be an issue for you; and less than 20 suggests it is probably not an issue for you.

The "Nudge" Test

Pause and listen to the Holy Spirit. Do you feel a "nudge" that perhaps you have sought identity, significance, security, or acceptance in your leadership?

Pray the following prayer in light of what God has shown you above:

Dear Heavenly Father,

I confess that I have sinned against You in how I have sought my identity, significance, security, and acceptance in leadership roles, positions, and titles rather than in my relationship with You. In particular, I confess that I have sought my identity, significance, security, or acceptance outside of You in the following ways: _____ (list what the Holy Spirit has shown you or brings to your mind now). I acknowledge that this is sin. Thank you that in Christ I am forgiven. I renounce seeking my identity, significance, security, and acceptance in these ways. I choose to base my life in You alone, through faith in Your Son Jesus Christ. Please fill me with Your Spirit and help me trust in You alone. Through Jesus Christ, my Lord. Amen.

Part 2 – Affirming Who We Are in Christ as Leaders

God loves us and wants us to be firmly rooted in Christ, and that must happen before we can freely lead others. Trying to discover who we are in leadership roles, and hoping such roles will make us more significant, secure, and accepted can only lead to disaster. On the other hand, leading others can be very fulfilling if we are deeply rooted in Christ. Read the following affirmations aloud and let the Word of God dwell richly within you:

My Identity In Christ Affirmed

I renounce the lie that I depend on any leadership role for my significance, because in Christ I am deeply significant. God says that:

I am the salt of the earth and the light of the world (see Matthew 5:13, 14)

I am a branch of the true vine, Jesus, a channel of His life (see John 15:1, 5)

I have been chosen and appointed by God to bear fruit (see John 15:16)

I am a personal, Spirit empowered witness for Christ (see Acts 1:8)

I am a temple of God (see 1 Corinthians 3:16)

I am a minister of reconciliation for God (see 2 Corinthians 5:17–21)

I am Christ's ambassador to the world (see 2 Corinthians 5:20)

I am God's fellow worker (see 2 Corinthians 6:1)

I am seated with Christ in the heavenly realm (see Ephesians 2:6)

I am God's workmanship, created for good works (see Ephesians 2:10)

I may approach God with freedom and confidence (see Ephesians 3:12)

I can do all things through Christ who strengthens me! (see Philippians 4:13)

I renounce the lie that I depend on any leadership role for my security, because in Christ I am totally secure. God says that:

I am free forever from condemnation (see Romans 8:1, 2)

I am assured that all things work together for good (see Romans 8:28)

I am free from any condemning charges against me (see Romans 8:31–34)

I cannot be separated from the love of God (see Romans 8:35–39)

I have been established, anointed, and sealed by God (see 2 Corinthians 1:21, 22)

I am confident that the good work God has begun in me will be perfected (see Philippians 1:6)

I am a citizen of heaven (see Philippians 3:20)

I am hidden with Christ in God (see Colossians 3:3)

I have not been given a spirit of cowardice, but of power, love, and a sound mind (see 2 Timothy 1:7)

I can find grace and mercy to help in time of need (see Hebrews 4:16)

I am born of God and the evil one cannot touch me. (see 1 John 5:18)

I renounce the lie that I depend on any leadership role for my acceptance, because in Christ I am completely accepted. God says that:

I am God's child (see John 1:12)

I am Christ's friend (see John 15:5)

I have been justified (see Romans 5:1)

I am united with the Lord and I am one spirit with Him (see 1 Corinthians 6:17)

I have been bought with a price: I belong to God (see 1 Corinthians 6:19, 20)

I am a member of Christ's body (see 1 Corinthians 12:27)

I am a saint, a holy one (see Ephesians 1:1)

I have been adopted as God's child (see Ephesians 1:5)

I have direct access to God through the Holy Spirit (see Ephesians 2:18)

I have been redeemed and forgiven of all my sins (see Colossians 1:14)

I am complete in Christ. (see Colossians 2:10)

My Identity In Christ Declared

Now get together with one other person. Sit or stand directly opposite each other. Each person should read the following aloud to the other person. One person in turn should read the entire list to the other person. (If you are working through the Leadership Steps on your own, try looking at yourself in a mirror as you read these statements.)

I declare to you, _____ (name), that you do not depend on any leadership role for your significance, because in Christ you are deeply significant. God says that:

You are the salt of the earth and the light of the world (see Matthew 5:13, 14)

You are a branch of the true vine, Jesus, a channel of His life (see John 15:1, 5)

You have been chosen and appointed by God to bear fruit (see John 15:16)

You are a personal, Spirit empowered witness for Christ (see Acts 1:8)

You are a temple of God (see 1 Corinthians 3:16)

You are a minister of reconciliation for God (see 2 Corinthians 5:17–21)

You are Christ's ambassador to the world (see 2 Corinthians 5:20)

You are God's fellow worker (see 2 Corinthians 6:1)

You are seated with Christ in the heavenly realm (see Ephesians 2:6)

You are God's workmanship, created for good works (see Ephesians 2:10)

You may approach God with freedom and confidence (see Ephesians 3:12)

You can do all things through Christ who strengthens you! (see Philippians 4:13)

I declare to you, _____ (name), that you do not depend on any leadership role for your security, because in Christ you are totally secure. God says that:

You are free forever from condemnation (see Romans 8:1,2)

You are assured that all things work together for good (see Romans 8:28)

You are free from any condemning charges against you (Romans 8:31–34)

You cannot be separated from the love of God (see Romans 8:35–39)

You have been established, anointed, and sealed by God (see 2 Corinthians 1:21, 22)

You are confident that the good work God has begun in you will be perfected (Philippians 1:6)

You are a citizen of heaven (see Philippians 3:20)

You are hidden with Christ in God (see Colossians 3:3)

You have not been given a spirit of cowardice, but of power, love, and a sound mind (see 2 Timothy 1:7)

You can find grace and mercy to help in time of need (see Hebrews 4:16)

You are born of God and the evil one cannot touch you. (see 1 John 5:18)

I declare to you, _____ (name), that you do not depend on any leadership role for your acceptance, because in Christ you are completely accepted. God says that:

You are God's child (see John 1:12)

You are Christ's friend (see John 15:5)

You have been justified (see Romans 5:1)

You are united with the Lord and you are one spirit with Him (see 1 Corinthians 6:17)

You have been bought with a price: You belong to God (see 1 Corinthians 6:19, 20)

You are a member of Christ's body (see 1 Corinthians 12:27)

You are a saint, a holy one (see Ephesians 1:1)

You have been adopted as God's child (see Ephesians 1:5)

You have direct access to God through the Holy Spirit (see Ephesians 2:18)

You have been redeemed and forgiven of all your sins (see Colossians 1:14)

You are complete in Christ. (see Colossians 2:10)

If you did the above with a partner, finish this step by praying for each other.

Step Two: Forgiveness in Leadership

Conflicts in leadership are inevitable. We will experience criticism, sabotage, ingratitude, and any number of pains and offences. Leaders who do not forgive will become bitter and angry and may ultimately experience burnout or other negative spiritual, mental, and physical outcomes.

Leaders must forgive others in order to relate to others in healthy ways and to maintain a healthy connection with both people and people-systems. However, we must forgive mainly for the sake of our own relationship with God (see Matthew 18:23–35). This Step will enable you to do that.

We are to forgive others as Christ has forgiven us. He did that by taking all the sins of the world upon Himself. Essentially, forgiving others is agreeing to live with the consequences of their sins. That may seem unfair, but we will have to anyway. The only real choice is to live in the bondage of bitterness, or forgive from our hearts others who have hurt us. It is for our own sake that we make that choice.

We forgive someone who has hurt us because the pain will not go away until we forgive. We don't heal damaged emotions in order to forgive. We forgive and our restored fellowship with God is what brings the healing.

Forgiveness does not mean tolerating sin. We have every right to set up scriptural boundaries to stop further abuse. Leaders who forgive their followers must still carry out discipline when appropriate. The difference is that they don't do it in the bitterness that would make it less effective.

Forgiveness does not necessarily mean that the other has done something wrong, but is merely an acknowledgement that the other has caused us pain. Of course, we do need to forgive when someone sins against us, but we also need to forgive when someone does something that is not sinful but causes us pain — such as when they give us godly correction.

As we forgive, we release the pain of what was said or done to us to God through Jesus Christ. Whenever the memory of what was said or done returns and causes pain again, we need to forgive again. As we continue to forgive, God will come and begin to heal the pain we have experienced. Forgiveness is not the same as reconciliation, although both are biblical concepts. If you have been wounded or sinned against, you have a responsibility to forgive (see Matthew 18:23-35 or Matthew 6:12-15). If you know you have wounded or sinned against someone else, you have a responsibility to seek reconciliation (see Matthew 5:23-26) – although either party may initiate reconciliation. As you go through this Step, the Lord might bring to your mind people with whom you need to initiate reconciliation. Make a list of them.

Begin with this prayer:

Dear Heavenly Father,

As a leader, I know that I have sinned many times. I have wounded others, knowingly and unknowingly. I thank You for the riches of Your kindness, forbearance, and patience towards me, knowing that Your kindness has led me to repentance. I confess that I have not shown that same kindness and patience towards those leaders or followers who have hurt or offended me. Instead, I have held on to my anger, bitterness, and resentment towards them. Please bring to my mind all the people I need to forgive who have wounded me either as a leader or a follower, in order that I may now choose to forgive. In Jesus' name. Amen.

(See Romans 2:4.)

List everyone the Lord brings to your mind – other leaders, followers, or anyone else who has wounded you:

Remember, it matters not whether these people have actually sinned against you. If you *feel* they have, the need to forgive them still exists. That is why many need to forgive God. Even though we know that God has not sinned, we may feel that He has let us down.

In order to forgive others from our hearts, we have to allow God to reach our emotional core and we need to acknowledge all hurtful and hateful feelings, especially the ones we have tried to suppress. God wants to surface such feelings so we can let them go. That happens when we forgive others for the specific things they have done that God brings to mind, and acknowledge how those things made us feel.

Forgiving yourself is actually acknowledging that God has forgiven you, but it is extremely helpful for some to say, "Lord I forgive myself for (tell God the mistakes you made and other things you are beating yourself up for)."

Forgiving others is a crisis of the will. Don't say, "Lord, I want to forgive" or "Lord, help me forgive". God will always help us. We *choose* to forgive people for specific things we believe they have done.

Pray the following prayer for each person on your list, and stay with that person until every painful memory has been acknowledged:

Lord, I choose to forgive _____(name) for _____(what they did or failed to do) which made me feel _____(describe the pain).

After you have prayed through your list, pray the following:

Lord, I choose not to hold on to my resentment. I renounce all bitterness. I give up my right to seek revenge or to punish those who have wounded me. I thank You for setting me free from my bondage to bitterness and I ask You to heal my damaged emotions. I choose to bless those who have hurt me. In particular, I choose to bless _____(name the people). In Jesus' name. Amen.

Reconciliation

List the names of all the people with whom you may need to seek reconciliation.

If we have sinned against another person, we need to go to that person and specifically ask them to forgive us for what we have done, or not done, and make restitution if it is called for (Matthew 5:23, 24). It is always better to do that personally rather than by letter, phone, or email. Begin the process of reconciliation now by praying as follows:

Almighty God, I confess that I sinned against _____(name of person) by _____(state what you did or said). By Your Holy Spirit, please show me how to seek reconciliation with this person. In Jesus' name I pray. Amen.

If you have said or done something that may have wounded the person but which was not necessarily sinful (such as speaking an appropriate word of correction), then use this prayer:

Dear Heavenly Father, I ask You to heal the wounds that I may have caused to _____(name of person) when I _____(state what you did or said). Please reveal to my mind any way that _____(state what you did or said) was sinful, so that I might repent. By Your Holy Spirit, please show me how to seek reconciliation with this person. In Jesus' name. Amen.

Be sure to follow through in any way the Lord shows you. Be patient in the process and note that reconciliation can never be guaranteed as it depends on the response of the other person (Romans 12:18). However, if you have forgiven them and sought their forgiveness, you will have peace with God. For much deeper discussion about reconciliation read Neil Anderson's book *Restoring Broken Relationships* (Bethany House Publishing, formerly *The Path to Reconciliation*, Regal Books).

Step Three: Overcoming Anxiety And Reactivity In Leadership

Anxiety disables leadership by immersing us in the problems and tensions around us in such a way that it prevents us from seeing God's truth and gaining perspective from God on how to move forward in obedience. Anxiety blinds leaders so that they lose any sense of vision and direction from God. Anxiety distorts our perspectives and our communication.

When leaders are anxious, they are more prone to reactive relationships: relationships where people instantly oppose one another and cease giving one another grace and forgiveness. In these relationships, we react out of our flesh instead of our spirits. Leaders can choose to respond thoughtfully and gracefully towards others who are reactive, especially those who oppose or criticize them personally. In order to do so, they must first recognize these relationships and choose to break the reactivity by responding in grace and love.

Part 1 – Overcoming Anxiety

Anxiety often operates in the background of our minds. The particular source(s) of anxiety may be any number of issues: too much to do; too much information to process; financial struggles; relationship struggles; problems at work; problems at home; etc. Often, several sources of anxiety may be operating at the same time. In order to overcome anxiety, we must ask the Holy Spirit to reveal the source(s) of anxiety. Then we need to repent of this anxiety, choosing to present the matter to God in prayer and thanksgiving. If the anxiety is deep-seated or chronic, we may need to do a "stronghold-busting" exercise to eliminate it (see the Freedom In Christ Discipleship Course for more information). To begin discerning anxiety in your life, pray the following:

Dear Heavenly Father,

You are the omniscient God. You know the thoughts and intentions of my heart. You know the situations I am in from the beginning to the end. I place my trust in You to supply all my needs according to Your riches in glory and to guide me into all truth. Please reveal to my mind all the emotions and symptoms that I have been experiencing which are evidence of anxiety in my life. In Jesus' name. Amen.

Tick the emotions and symptoms of anxiety below that are true for you. Add others that the Spirit brings to mind.

- ❑ General uneasiness or nervousness
- ❑ Impulsiveness
- ❑ Unforgiveness
- ❑ Defensiveness
- ❑ Lack of concentration
- ❑ Restlessness
- ❑ Hyperactivity
- ❑ Loss of creativity
- ❑ Not thinking clearly
- ❑ Highly emotional
- ❑ Loss of objectivity
- ❑ Procrastination
- ❑ Stubbornness
- ❑ Sense of helplessness or self-doubt
- ❑ Difficulty in making choices
- ❑ Vivid nightmares
- ❑ Blaming
- ❑ Criticism and judgmentalism
- ❑ Wilfulness
- ❑ Demanding your own way
- ❑ Gossip or rumours
- ❑ Feeling victimized
- ❑ Exaggeration
- ❑ Moodiness
- ❑ Miscommunication
- ❑ Too much TV or media
- ❑ Too much drink or food
- ❑ Money concerns
- ❑ Working too hard
- ❑ Others:

Selecting more than three indicates that anxiety may be a problem. More than seven suggests that you may be chronically anxious.

Pray the following prayer:

Loving Father,

Your Word tells us not to be anxious, but I realize that I have not obeyed Your Word. I have allowed myself to be anxious about many things, as the emotions and symptoms above have shown me. I confess that my anxiety shows a lack of trust in You. I now ask You to search me, O God, and know my heart; try me and know my anxious thoughts; and see if there be any hurtful way in me, and lead me in the everlasting way. Please reveal to my mind all sources of anxiety that I might commit each of them to You in trust and obedience. In Jesus' precious name. Amen.

(Matthew 6:31–34; Philippians 4:6; Psalm 139:23, 24)

1. List the sources of anxiety (evidenced by the emotions and symptoms above) that the Holy Spirit reveals to your mind, being as specific as possible:

(Example: I have so much to do that I'm afraid I will miss something important.)

2. For each source of anxiety, describe what You are believing or assuming (these are generally "lies") that is causing you apprehension or emotional pain.

(Example: I need to do everything I'm doing.)

Respond with this prayer:

Dear Heavenly Father,

I choose to trust in You alone. I do not trust in myself or my own abilities to resolve the situations in my life. I do not trust in my relatives and friends to resolve the situations in my life. I do not trust in my work to resolve the situations in my life. I do not trust my church to resolve the situations in my life. I choose to trust in You alone. I now commit the following sources of anxiety to You in prayer:

1. List the anxiety or source of anxiety.

2. Describe the emotions or symptoms that accompany it.

3. Pray for the appropriate resolution or outcome.

In the name of Jesus Christ, I now renounce the lies that I have believed about these sources of anxiety. In particular, I renounce the lie that:
_____(list each lie you have believed or assumed).

Thank You that You are sovereign over my life. Thank You that You are in control of the situations of my life. Thank You that You always work for my good in every situation. Thank You that through Jesus Christ I am not a victim of anxiety, but I am an overcomer of anxiety. I choose to walk in obedience to You, resisting anxiety by keeping my focus on You. Through Jesus Christ. Amen.

Part 2 – Breaking Cycles Of Reactivity

Reactivity cycles occur whenever we become stuck in a relationship where we are opposing, resisting, and criticizing the other. We become reactive when we begin to engage with other people out of our flesh, that sinful aspect of our humanity that resists God's will. When we are reactive, others often become reactive to us as well, entrapping us in a reactivity cycle.

We may become reactive not only towards individuals, but also towards groups and organizations. For example, people can become reactive towards a political party, so that no matter what the leader of a certain political party might say these people will find something to oppose. This may lead to intractable disagreements among people regarding politics, which prevent people from working together for the good of their country.

At any time, we can break reactivity cycles by persistently choosing to respond to the other out of grace, love, and forgiveness. Respond to God as you pray this prayer:

Dear Heavenly Father,

Your Word says that You are merciful and gracious, slow to anger, and abounding in steadfast love (Exodus 34:6). Although I have received Your mercy, I confess that I have not always extended this mercy to others. Instead, I have allowed myself to react out of my flesh. Please reveal to my mind anyone with whom I have been reactive, so that I might repent and find freedom. In Jesus' name. Amen.

1. List each person that the Spirit brings to Your mind.

2. For each person, describe how you have been reactive towards that person.

3. For each person, pray the following prayer:

Lord,

I confess that I have been reactive towards _____ (name the person or group) by _____ (describe the ways in which you have been reactive). Thank You that in Christ I am forgiven. I now choose to respond to _____ (name the person or group) in grace, love, and mercy. I choose to give _____ (name the person or group) grace as You have given grace to me through Your Son Jesus Christ. I ask that You would make me an agent of reconciliation with (name the person or group). I choose to bless (name the person or group) in the name of Jesus Christ, my Lord. Amen.

(Ephesians 4:32)

As appropriate, you may need to seek reconciliation with those on your list (see Step 2). Allow the Holy Spirit to lead you in this. Often, as we choose to break the cycle of reactivity, reconciliation with that person naturally begins to occur by the Holy Spirit.

Step Four: Embracing Our Leadership Responsibility

The purpose of this Step is to help us understand and embrace who God has created us to be as leaders, whether we are a natural leader, a leader in our people-system, or a leader in a particular situation. Natural leaders are people who lead as a matter of course, no matter what context they seem to be in. Their normal disposition is leadership. Other leaders may be called to lead in a particular people-system (group of people). They may be leaders at home or at work, but they do not generally lead outside their people-system. Almost everyone will need to lead from time to time as the situation requires. Because almost everyone will lead from time to time, there is not an activity for discernment in this aspect of leadership.

After helping identify how you are called to leadership, this Step then helps you resolve the times when you have failed to exercise leadership or when you have exercised leadership in the wrong way. If we fail to lead as God requires or if we exercise our leadership in the wrong way, then we have sinned. So we must resolve these areas of sin if we are to lead appropriately.

Part 1 – Identifying The Scope Of Your Leadership

Dear Heavenly Father,

I rejoice that You have saved me by grace through faith, and that I am Your workmanship created in Christ Jesus for good works that You have prepared for me (Ephesians 2:8–10). I know that You have created each person differently, and You have given each person different spiritual gifts, callings, and ministries by Your Holy Spirit (1 Corinthians 12:4–7). I pray that You would reveal to my mind how you have created me and called me to lead. In Jesus' name. Amen.

Natural Leadership

Please rate the following statements on a scale of 1 to 10, with 10 being the highest:

- No matter whether I am at work, church, home, or other organizations, I find that people consistently ask me to lead.
- Whenever I am leading, I feel confident.
- Whenever I am leading, I feel positive.
- Whenever I am leading, I feel energized.
- I usually serve more effectively by leading a team than I do as a general team member.
- I generally do not feel threatened or jealous when I am around other leaders.
- People seem to enjoy following my leadership.
- The best way I can serve people is by leading them.
- I find it relatively easy to get a clear vision from God for my work, church, home, or other organization of which I am part.
- I can point to a record of good fruit stemming from contexts in which I was leading.
- **Total**

If your score is 70 or above, it is likely that God has called you as a natural leader. (It is often best to verify your responses with your spouse or a close friend, who can assist you in your discernment.)

Once you have completed this exercise, pray the following:

Dear Heavenly Father,

Thank you for creating me to be the leader that I am, whether or not I am a natural leader. I surrender to Your purpose in my life regarding leadership. I affirm that Your Son Jesus was the greatest leader of all, the perfect example of genuine leadership. By Your Spirit, I choose to follow His example of leadership, using leadership to serve others in humility. May my leadership always reflect and be filled with the life of Jesus. Amen.

People-System Leadership

Review the list of people-systems below. Put a tick next to those in which you already serve as a leader or you believe God is calling you to serve as a leader. Write a note next to any people-system that requires additional specification (e.g. "budget team at work" or "Girl Guides troop").

- ❑ Your immediate family
- ❑ Your extended family
- ❑ Your work
- ❑ Teams or other groups at work
- ❑ Your profession or professional associations
- ❑ Your church
- ❑ Church cell group/home group
- ❑ Community and social organizations
- ❑ Others:

Pray the following in light of your answers above:

Dear Heavenly Father,

I thank You for the person You have created me to be. I now freely and wholeheartedly choose to walk in the ways You have prepared for me, accepting the leadership responsibilities You have given me. In particular, I affirm that You have called me to lead in _____(list all specific contexts). By Your Holy Spirit, empower me to serve others through my leadership in whatever people-systems or situations You place me, so that I might bring glory and honour to my Lord Jesus Christ. Amen.

Part 2 – Identifying Situations And People-Systems In Which You Failed To Lead

Every leader makes mistakes; every leader fails. This part of the Step focuses on times when we have neglected our leadership responsibilities or times in which we sought to fulfil our leadership responsibilities in a sinful way. Begin by praying the following prayer:

Dear Heavenly Father,

I thank you for Your mercy and kindness, knowing that Your kindness leads me to repentance (Romans 2:4). I confess that I have not always led when I have needed to lead, neglecting my responsibility before You. I also confess that I have not always led in the way I should lead, but have led out of selfish motives and in sinful ways. Please reveal to my mind any and all ways that I have not led as You have wanted, so that I might repent. In Jesus' name. Amen.

1. List the people-systems above in which you have failed to lead as God wanted:

2. List the situations in which you have neglected your leadership responsibilities or have failed to lead as needed:

3. List the situations in which you have led wrongly:

4. Put a mark next to any of the following that are true for you:

- ❏ I have used guilt or shame to get others to do what I want or think best.
- ❏ I have demanded that others do what I want or follow my rules.
- ❏ I have controlled others by my strong personality, heavy-handed persuasion, or the use of fear or intimidation.
- ❏ I have expected to be in charge because I am the leader.
- ❏ I have tried to get others to do what I want using rules, regulations, and standards.
- ❏ I have striven to get or maintain a position or role in order to accomplish my agenda.
- ❏ I have assumed responsibility for the lives and well-being of other adults under my leadership.
- ❏ I have driven others and myself harder and harder in order to achieve the vision.
- ❏ I have been stubborn and rigid in my leadership.
- ❏ I have required people under my leadership to do what I say, when I say it and how I say it.
- ❏ I have expected others to work as hard as I do if they want my approval.
- ❏ I have never been really satisfied with the performance of others I lead.
- ❏ Other things the Lord may show you:

Pray the following prayer, including the items you have listed above:

Lord, I confess that I have not led when I should have. Specifically, I confess my sins in these areas: _____(list the ones indicated in 1 and 2 above). I also confess that I have led wrongly. Specifically, I confess these wrong ways of leading: _____(list the ones indicated in 3 or 4 above). Thank You that in Jesus Christ I am forgiven. I now commit myself to leading in whatever situation You ask and in a manner worthy of Jesus Christ, the greatest leader of all. Amen.

Conclude this Step with the following prayer:

Gracious and loving God,

Thank You for allowing me to serve people through leadership as the person I am in Christ. I pray that I might fulfil all my leadership responsibilities humbly, joyfully, and lovingly, in the manner of Your Son, Jesus. Empower me by Your Holy Spirit to live in obedience to You and serve in love. Through Jesus Christ. Amen.

Step Five: Money, Sex, And Power In Leadership

When a leader fails, most often it is because of one (or more) of the following: money, sex, and power. When any of these three things are out of balance in our lives, it will undermine our leadership ability. This will be true even if the issue does not seem to be directly related to our leadership context. This Step asks the Holy Spirit to reveal to our minds all ways that we have sinned or are sinning in each of these areas.

Part 1 – Money

When we use the term "money", we are referring to all the financial and material resources (car, home, computer, etc.) God has provided for us. In this Step, we are asking God to reveal not only our behaviours but also our attitudes concerning our financial and material resources. Greed is the desire to have more and more or to have more than you actually need. Covetousness is the longing to possess things that other people have. Envy is a feeling of discontent or resentful longing arising from someone else's situation.

Begin with this prayer:

Dear Heavenly Father,

I thank You that You richly supply me with all the resources I need through Your Son Jesus Christ. You have said that the love of money is the root of all kinds of evil (1 Timothy 6:10). Because of this, You have told us to keep our lives free from the love of money and choose to be content with what we have (Hebrews 13:5). You have promised that if we seek first Your kingdom, then You would add to us all the things we need (Matthew 6:33). I confess that I have not always done this. Instead, I have sinned through greed, envy, and covetousness. I have also sinned by failing to be a good steward of the financial and material resources that You have supplied to me. I now ask You to reveal to my mind any and all ways that I have sinned regarding money, that I might fully repent. In Jesus' name. Amen.

Ways that we may sin as leaders regarding money:

- ☐ Failing to live within my means or according to a budget
- ☐ Not paying off my credit cards each month or carrying a large balance on my credit cards with no ability to pay them off
- ☐ Having large amounts of consumer debt
- ☐ Taking small items from my workplace for my personal use
- ☐ Failing to file or pay my taxes on time and in full
- ☐ Trying to disguise money problems that I may be having
- ☐ Failing to exercise good stewardship of the resources God has given me (e.g. failing to maintain my car or my home, failing to care for my computer and phone, etc.)
- ☐ Using or administering the financial resources of my workplace without transparency and appropriate financial controls
- ☐ Failing to insist that others use appropriate financial controls and stewardship of our common resources (at home, in the workplace, or in church)
- ☐ Ignoring financial practices that I know to be wrong (for myself, at home, in the workplace, or in church)
- ☐ Feeling rebellious or defensive when I'm asked to give appropriate account for my financial activities and expenditures
- ☐ Failing to ensure that my current account and savings account balance each month
- ☐ Finding myself practising "retail therapy" or conspicuous consumption
- ☐ Envying or coveting the resources of other friends, co-workers or leaders in similar situations to myself
- ☐ Finding it difficult to share my financial needs with others who may be able to help me
- ☐ Failing to give financially as God has instructed me
- ☐ Spending a lot of time thinking and worrying about money matters
- ☐ Being overly concerned about getting the financial remuneration that I feel I deserve
- ☐ Feeling that I am entitled to a certain level of financial remuneration
- ☐ Other ways that God is showing me:

Respond to what God has shown you by praying this prayer:

Dear Heavenly Father,

I thank You for the riches of Your kindness towards me, leading me to turn away from my sin. I confess that I have sinned regarding money in the following ways: _____ (list them). Thank You that in Jesus Christ I am forgiven. I choose to turn away from my sin and exercise good stewardship over the financial and material resources that You have entrusted to me as a person and as a leader. Help me to be faithful in little, so that I may receive much to use for Your kingdom (Luke 16:10–12). Through Jesus, my Lord. Amen.

Part 2 – Sex

In this section, we are not looking to deal with all the ways that we have sinned regarding sex, but we are focusing primarily on our leadership context. However, it is important that we repent of all immoral sexual activity according to the Bible and ensure that we resolve all outstanding personal and spiritual issues regarding our sexuality. (See *The Steps To Freedom In Christ*, Step 6, for guidance on how to resolve issues regarding immoral sexual activity more fully.) In this Step, we are asking God to reveal not only our behaviours but also our attitudes regarding sexual issues.

Pray the following:

Dear Heavenly Father,

I thank You that sex is Your good gift to be exercised according to Your Word in the covenant of marriage between one man and one woman. I acknowledge that immoral sexual activity includes a range of sins that undermine our relationship with You and with others. I confess that it ruins our ability to lead as Christians. I now ask You to bring to my mind any sexual sin in thought, word, or action that I might repent of these sexual sins and break their bondages. In Jesus' name. Amen.

Ways that we may sin as leaders regarding sex:

- ☐ Thinking about co-workers or those I lead in a lustful way
- ☐ Looking at co-workers or those I lead in a lustful way
- ☐ Looking at pornography
- ☐ "Channel surfing" or internet surfing when I am tired or stressed
- ☐ Watching films and TV programmes that contain strong sexual images
- ☐ Daydreaming about immoral sexual activity
- ☐ Finding myself longing to spend time with people of the opposite gender (who I am not either dating or married to), especially in one-to-one circumstances
- ☐ Not taking time to develop healthy friendships with people of the same gender
- ☐ Thinking too much about past relationships, especially if they involved immoral sexual contact
- ☐ Dwelling on temptations towards homosexuality or paedophilia
- ☐ Not giving sufficient attention and effort to nurturing my sexual relationship with my spouse
- ☐ Using sex with my spouse as a means of fulfilling my sinful lust
- ☐ Other ways that God is showing me:

Once you have considered this list, choose to repent by praying this prayer:

Dear Heavenly Father,

I admit that I have not always exercised self-control and obedience to You and Your Word regarding my sexuality. I confess that I have sinned against You by _____ (list them). I renounce all these sexual sins, and I admit to any wilful participation. I choose now to present my eyes, mouth, mind, heart, hands, feet, and sexual organs to You as instruments of righteousness. I present my whole body to You as a living sacrifice, holy and acceptable. I choose to reserve the sexual use of my body for marriage only (see Hebrews 13:4). I now loose myself from any sinful bonds I have made with any co-worker or follower in my heart or in my behaviour. In the name of the Lord Jesus Christ, I cancel any effects my sin has on my leadership and take back any ground I have given to the

devil. Thank You that You have totally cleansed and forgiven me and that You love and accept me just the way I am. Therefore, I choose now to present myself and my body to You as clean in Your eyes. In Jesus' name. Amen.

Part 3 – Power

Power is a complex concept in leadership. Leaders have authority and responsibility for people in order that people may experience God's best for them. However, as leaders we can often use our authority and responsibility as a means to control and manipulate others. Most leaders unintentionally fall into this from time to time. A few leaders consciously choose to control others. Some leaders will try to control others because they enjoy having positions of power and influence. Other leaders try to control people out of fear and self-protection. Some people will seek positions of leadership in order to use these positions of leadership to achieve their own desires or their own agenda.

In this section, we are asking God to reveal to us all the ways that we have sought to control or manipulate people using our leadership. Begin with this prayer:

Almighty God, You are the Sovereign Lord of all creation. We know that nothing is outside the control of Your Son Jesus Christ, even though it does not always seem that everything is under His control. Lord Jesus, You uphold the universe by Your power. As Your people, the power we have comes by Your Holy Spirit and through godliness. Your power is at work within us, but it enables us to live fully for You. You have not given us power over others. It is the love of Christ that controls us, and You do not allow us to control others. Instead, You call us to self-control. I confess that I have used my leadership as a means to gain or exercise power over others. I repent of this sin and ask You to reveal to my mind all the ways that I have used my leadership as a means to control others. Please reveal all the ways that I have become intoxicated with my power and position over others. In Jesus' name. Amen.

(See Hebrews 2:8; Hebrews 1:3; 2 Timothy 3:5; 2 Timothy 1:7; Ephesians 3:20; 2 Corinthians 5:14.)

Ways that we may sin as leaders regarding power and control:

- ❏ Expecting (or trying to force) people to follow me because of my position, title, degrees, or achievements
- ❏ Using guilt or shame to persuade others to do what I think is right
- ❏ Using biblical verses such as "Touch not my anointed ones" (Psalm 105:15) to defend myself or persuade others
- ❏ Not sharing requested or needed information in an open and timely manner
- ❏ Withholding pertinent information needed by my co-workers or followers
- ❏ Acting or speaking in deceptive ways in order to control others or protect myself
- ❏ Spending time and energy trying to control people and situations instead of exercising self-control
- ❏ Using harsh or judgmental language with others, especially when I want them to do something
- ❏ Threatening others with bad consequences in order to get my way
- ❏ Threatening others with my own resignation or withdrawal in order to get my way
- ❏ Having the tendency to think that my way is the right way
- ❏ Giving people responsibility but expecting them to fulfil it in the way I determine
- ❏ Not allowing, actively or passively, other people to take leadership responsibility as appropriate
- ❏ Not giving people open access to the resources needed in order to fulfil their responsibilities fully and in a timely way
- ❏ Giving different people different information about the same activity, responsibility or situation
- ❏ Using rules, regulations, or the Bible in a way that stifles discussion and tries to force people to listen to me or obey me
- ❏ Using phrases such as "because I said so" or "the Lord told me" when people raise questions about my decisions or opinions
- ❏ Using technical, obscure or complicated language in order to persuade people that I am right
- ❏ Being harsh, critical, or abusive with others, especially if they do not agree with me
- ❏ Taking responsibility for someone else's obedience and discipleship
- ❏ Other ways that God may be showing you:

Pray the following:

Almighty God,

I confess that I have used my leadership as a means to control people and situations. In particular, I confess _____ (list them). I renounce all ways and means of using leadership to control others, especially the ones that I have listed. Thank You that in Jesus I am forgiven. I cancel all ground gained in my life through my sin in this area. I choose to lead in the way of Jesus, who for our sakes emptied Himself and made Himself nothing, becoming the servant of all (Philippians 2:5ff.). Fill me with Your Holy Spirit, that I might live for You. In Jesus' name. Amen.

Step Six: Renouncing Pride, Defensiveness, And Selfish Ambition In Leadership

This Step addresses three key areas that deeply affect leadership: pride, defensiveness, and selfish ambition. These three factors are at the root of the lack of healthy unity, not only in the Church but also in the workplace. These factors cause a lot of dysfunction and disease among leaders as well as followers. They prevent people and people-systems from working together effectively for the benefit of society.

Part 1 – Pride

Pride is one of the great leadership sins. Pride involves having a high opinion of oneself or one's importance, which can show itself in many ways. Pride often puts leaders in situations where people will oppose, resist, or resent them. Pride always puts leaders in opposition to God. Left unchecked, pride functions like a cancer in leadership, eating away at our leadership until it dies. Even many secular books and authorities on leadership recognize the destructive influence of pride in a leader.

Begin with the following prayer:

Dear Heavenly Father, You have said that pride goes before destruction and an arrogant spirit before a fall. As a leader, I confess that I have often considered myself more highly than I ought. I have wanted to be first and not last. I have chosen to serve myself, seeking my own desires and disguising it as serving others. As a result, I have given ground to the devil in my life and I have compromised my leadership. I have sinned by believing I could know and choose what is best for others on my own. In so doing, I have placed my will before Yours, and I have centred my life around myself instead of You.

I repent of my pride and selfishness in leadership and pray that all ground gained in me by the enemies of the Lord Jesus Christ would be cancelled. I choose to rely on the Holy Spirit's power and guidance so I will do nothing from selfishness or empty conceit. With humility of mind, I will seek to lead by Your Holy Spirit with the love and grace of Jesus.

Please show me now all the specific ways in which I have led in pride. Enable me through love to serve others and in honour to prefer others. I ask all of this in the gentle and humble name of Jesus, my Lord. Amen.

(See Proverbs 16:18; Matthew 6:33; 16:24; Romans 12:10; Philippians 2:3.)

Allow the Holy Spirit to show you any specific ways in which pride has infected your leadership. As the Lord brings to your mind areas of pride, use the prayer below to guide you in your confession.

Ways that pride might become evident in leadership:

- ☐ Having or showing a stubborn and determined intention to do what I think is best
- ☐ Leading from my own understanding and experience rather than patiently seeking God's guidance through prayer and His Word
- ☐ Leading from my own energy and effort instead of depending on the power of the Holy Spirit
- ☐ Leading in ways that control or manipulate others instead of using self-control
- ☐ Having impatience when it comes to seeing the change or getting the outcomes I want in my leadership contexts
- ☐ Being too busy doing important things as a leader to take time to do little things for others
- ☐ Having a tendency to think that I do not need anyone's help to lead
- ☐ Finding it hard to admit when I am wrong
- ☐ Being more concerned about pleasing people than pleasing God with my leadership
- ☐ Being concerned about getting the credit I feel I deserve as a leader
- ☐ Thinking that as a leader I am more humble, spiritual, religious, or devoted than others
- ☐ Being driven to obtain recognition for my leadership abilities, especially because of the size or scope of my leadership responsibilities
- ☐ Feeling that my needs are not as important as others' needs so that I must sacrifice myself
- ☐ Feeling that others do not have the same level of commitment or ability in leadership as me
- ☐ Often feeling that if I do not do something as a leader then no one else will
- ☐ Thinking that I must keep things going as a leader otherwise they may fall apart

- ❑ Considering myself better than others because of my accomplishments or position as a leader
- ❑ Other ways I have thought more highly of myself than I should:

For each of the above areas that has been true in your life, pray:

Lord, I agree I have been proud by _____(list the ways). Thank You for forgiving me for my pride. I choose to renounce pride and humble myself before You and others. I choose to place all my confidence in You and none in my flesh. In Jesus' name. Amen.

Part 2 – Defending Ourselves Wrongly

Self-defence can be another sign of pride in a leader, or it may reflect that the leader is seeking his or her significance, security or acceptance in leadership. Self-defence is always problematic: if we have done something wrong, we have no defence; if we have not done anything wrong, we need no defence because God will defend us. Defensiveness will always undermine leadership, especially by undermining other people's trust in the leader. Pray the following:

Dear Heavenly Father,

You have promised to be my shelter and my fortress. By Your grace, You surround me and defend me. I admit that I have not always trusted in You as my defender. Instead, because of pride or insecurity, I have often struggled as a leader to admit that I was wrong or that I made a mistake. I have resisted attempts by others to show me my faults in accordance with Your Word. I have chosen to defend myself wrongly. In so doing I have wounded others and myself and I have offended You. Please reveal to my mind any ways that I have failed to trust You by trying to defend myself wrongly. In the name of Jesus. Amen.

Ways we defend ourselves wrongly:

- ❏ Pretending or thinking that I have not done anything wrong
- ❏ Pretending or thinking that my behaviour is better than it really is
- ❏ Focusing on my own best motives and another's worst behaviours
- ❏ Denying or distorting reality, evidence, or the truth
- ❏ Retreating into entertainment, drugs, alcohol, or food
- ❏ Trying to portray myself in a better light than others
- ❏ Withdrawing from people or keeping people at a distance
- ❏ Regressing to less threatening times or to immature attitudes and behaviours
- ❏ Showing displaced anger or irritability
- ❏ Projecting my problems on to others; blaming others for my problems; shifting the focus on to others
- ❏ Rationalizing my behaviour or my circumstances
- ❏ Lying, disguising the truth, or giving partial truths
- ❏ Presenting a false image of myself or my motives
- ❏ Framing motives, behaviours, attitudes, and situations in ways that are deceptive or that present myself as better than I am
- ❏ Adopting a martyr complex
- ❏ Adopting a messiah complex
- ❏ Adopting a hermit complex
- ❏ Showing a lack of openness and transparency
- ❏ Refusing to trust and release others
- ❏ Other ways that the Holy Spirit may show you:

In light of the above, pray the following:

Gracious Lord,

I confess that I have defended myself wrongly by _____ (list them). Thank You for Your forgiveness. I choose to trust You to defend and protect me. In Jesus' name. Amen.

Part 3 – Selfish Ambition, Envy, And Jealousy

Envy, jealousy and selfish ambition are three related sins. They lead to unholy comparisons with others and unrighteous competition. These sins are related to the sin of pride (see Philippians 2:3). In a sense, jealousy is an intensification of envy, and selfish ambition is an intensification of jealousy. This part of the Step seeks to reveal these sins in our lives so that we might repent.

There are four primary sources of envy, jealousy, and selfish ambition. First, people may feel or fear that they are being displaced in terms of their relationships with others or in terms of their status (position or influence) in their leadership context. Second, feeling insecure (or having our sense of security in someone other than Jesus) may lead to these sins. Third, people may develop an entitlement mentality, believing that they deserve something (especially something someone else has) because of their own efforts. Finally, these sins may result from an unwillingness to pay the price for – or trying to find a shortcut to get – what one wants. All these flow from pride and conceit. They may all be corrected by finding our significance, security, and acceptance in Jesus rather than our leadership.

Envy

Envy is a feeling of discontent or resentful longing aroused by someone else's possessions, qualities, or circumstances – including God's blessings. Envy is related to covetousness. Envy refers to wanting what someone else has. Ultimately, it will seek to destroy the one who is envied. Envy leads to rivalry, divisions, and quarrels (see Mark 15:10; Galatians 5:18–21; Philippians 1:15). Pray the following:

Dear Heavenly Father,

You have promised to supply all our needs according to Your riches in glory in Christ Jesus. You have commanded us not to desire what others have, whether it is relationships or property, talents or resources. Such envy is a work of the flesh, not the Spirit. I confess that as a leader I have often envied what other leaders have. I ask You to reveal to my mind all the ways that I have envied others, so that I might repent. In Jesus' name. Amen. (See Philippians 4:19; Exodus 20:17; Galatians 5:21.)

Some ways that we envy as leaders:

- ❑ Longing for the financial resources of another
- ❑ Longing for the material resources of another
- ❑ Feeling that if I only had what someone else had, then I would be successful or happy
- ❑ Longing for the relationships of another
- ❑ Longing to be like another in terms of talents, abilities, spiritual gifts, skills
- ❑ Longing for the leadership position of another
- ❑ Feeling resentful towards others because of what they have
- ❑ Not feeling content with what God has provided me
- ❑ Feeling that I need to work harder or smarter in order to get what others have
- ❑ Other ways the Holy Spirit may show you:

Once you have considered the items above, pray the following:

Gracious God,

I confess that I have sinned by envying others. Specifically, I have envied others by: _____ (list them, being as specific as possible). I repent of my envy. Thank You that in Jesus I am forgiven. I ask You to wash me clean from the stain of envy. I choose to trust You and rejoice in Your provision for me. I choose to be content with what I have, knowing that You will use what I have to bring glory to Your Son Jesus. In His name I pray. Amen.

Jealousy

Jealousy is feeling or showing resentment towards someone because of that person's achievements, successes, perceived advantages, or relationships. Whereas envy focuses on what another has, jealousy focuses on the other person. Like envy, jealousy usually leads to quarrels and strife. Left unchecked, jealousy becomes an unholy zeal directed against another.

(There is a holy jealousy based on covenant faithfulness. This jealousy is aroused when someone gives to another the loyalty and affection belonging to one in covenant relationship. For example, when God's people worship idols or when a wife has affections for a man not her husband. See Exodus 20:5.)

Begin with this prayer:

Holy God,

Your Word says that You are a jealous God, calling us to a faithful love for You. At the same time, Your Word says that jealousy in us is a work of the flesh leading to arguments and dissensions. I confess that I have often resented other leaders because of their positions and accomplishments. I have sometimes even harboured ill will against them. This is sin. I ask You to reveal to my mind all the ways that I have been jealous and all the people of whom I have been jealous, so that I might repent. Through Jesus Christ, my Lord. Amen.

Ways that we can be jealous as leaders:

- ❑ Feeling that if I only had the same advantages as other leaders then I would have their accomplishments
- ❑ Feeling resentment towards others because of the relationships they have or enjoy
- ❑ Having hard feelings towards others because they have unfair advantages over me
- ❑ Feeling discontented because of the successes of others
- ❑ Secretly hoping that another leader would fail
- ❑ Feeling disgruntled with God because of the relationships others seem to enjoy with Him
- ❑ Other ways the Holy Spirit may show you:

People of whom I have been jealous:

Write the names of people and organizations the Lord shows you.

Reflecting on your answers above, pray this prayer:

Almighty God,

I confess that I have committed the sin of jealousy. I confess that I have been jealous by _____ (list them). Thank You that in Jesus Christ I am forgiven. Cleanse me completely from the sin of jealousy.

I now ask You to bless abundantly all those I have been jealous of: _____ (list the people). I ask You to heal any relationships broken because of jealousy, especially my relationship with _____ (list them).

Thank You for saving me by Your grace. Thank You for who I am in Your Son, Jesus Christ. Thank You that I am Your child and that You love me fully and completely. I rejoice in Your love for me. I choose now to walk in the good works that You have prepared for me to do. Help me love You faithfully. Through Jesus. Amen.

Selfish Ambition

Zeal or ambition can be a good trait in a leader. Leaders with a healthy sense of ambition will seek to achieve great things for God, for people and for their organizations. Such zeal is a healthy, godly quality that inspires leaders for excellence. Leaders with a healthy sense of ambition will not care who gets the credit as long as the godly outcomes are achieved. Leaders with a healthy zeal will put others first and promote their well-being.

Selfish ambition is not the same as healthy ambition. Selfish ambition is a desire to put oneself forward as deserving of something someone else has. It flows from envy and jealousy. It is self-seeking instead of serving others. Selfish ambition is a partisan and factious spirit that will do almost anything to get its way and to get ahead. As such, selfish ambition always leads to a sense of rivalry and unholy competition with others. Selfish ambition is always destructive, leading to many evil practices (see James 3:14–16). When leaders become selfishly ambitious, they ultimately destroy themselves, other people, and sometimes the very organizations they lead.

Pray this prayer for discernment of selfish ambition in your life:

Loving Father,

You have told us to do nothing out of selfish ambition or vain conceit, but in humility of mind to count others as more significant (Philippians 2:3). I know that in Christ I am significant. However, I have repeatedly tried to find my sense of significance in other things. I confess that I have often sought my sense of significance in comparison and in competition with other leaders. I have allowed envy or jealousy to lead to a spirit of rivalry. This is sin. Please reveal to me all the ways that I have been selfishly ambitious, that I may repent. Also reveal to my mind all those with whom I have had an unhealthy rivalry and sense of competition. Through Jesus, my Lord. Amen.

Ways selfish ambition can manifest in our lives:

- ❑ Having a strong sense of competition regarding something that is not normally competitive (such as a game or a sport)
- ❑ Striving against another person
- ❑ Acting in ways that seem to set people against each other or seem to create disunity
- ❑ Comparing oneself with others in terms of numbers and quantities (e.g. size of budget, number of church members, scope of responsibilities)
- ❑ Thinking myself significant because I have a larger _____ (ministry, budget, workload, membership, etc.) than another leader
- ❑ Speaking or acting in ways that criticize, undermine, disparage, tear down, or in other ways harm another leader or his/her organization, ministry, achievements, etc.
- ❑ Speaking or acting in ways that harm another leader's relationships
- ❑ Other ways the Holy Spirit may show you:

List all the leaders and organizations with which you have developed an unhealthy rivalry or sense of competition:

Using your answers above, pray this prayer:

Gracious God,

Although I have been created and called by You for leadership, I have not led as You desire. I realize that I have not led by the wisdom that is pure, peaceable, gentle, open to reason, full of mercy and good fruits, impartial, and sincere (James 3:14–17). Instead, I have harboured selfish ambition in my heart by: _____ (list them). In all these ways I have sought to put myself forward and advance my own agenda. I have not served others, but I have harmed others with my competition and rivalry. Thank You that in Christ I am forgiven. I ask You to cleanse me completely from every trace of selfish ambition. I ask You to bless and give success to all the other leaders around me, in particular _____ (list them). I pray that You would heal any damage I have done through my selfish ambition. By the grace of Jesus. Amen.

The Holy Spirit may ask you to go to leaders in connection with whom you have had selfish ambition in order to seek reconciliation and in order to bless that leader.

Close this Step with this declaration:

I here and now, in the name and authority of the Lord Jesus Christ, renounce all envy, jealousy, and selfish ambition. I choose to rejoice in God's provision for me, in the person God has made me to be as His child, and in where God has called and placed me as a leader (Luke 10:20). In Jesus' name, I cancel all ground gained by Satan in my life, my leadership, my ministry, my work, and the organizations of which I am part because of my envy, jealousy, and selfish ambition. In Jesus' name, I now break every unholy bond I have created with people _____ (list any that come to mind) through envy, jealousy, and selfish ambition.

In humility, I now choose to consider others more significant than myself. I choose to honour God and honour other leaders. I choose to rest in God's sovereignty over my life and my leadership, rejoicing that my name is written in heaven. Amen.

Note: If you are using the accompanying DVD to go through this process, the notes for the talk that introduces Step 7 are on pages 129–132.

Step Seven: Choosing Faith For Leading

Unbelief is another sin that acts like a cancer for leadership. Unbelief is not the same as doubt. Doubt, a sense of uncertainty, is common to all people. The Bible tells us to be merciful to those who doubt (Jude 22). Unbelief is the opposite of faith, resistant and hostile towards belief. Unbelief undermines our confidence in God and leads us away from the truth. Unbelief blinds our minds and hardens our hearts. As leaders we must repent of our unbelief and be transformed by the renewing of our minds.

Faith is a state and act of believing on the basis of the reliability of the one trusted. Faith depends on relationship with the object of faith. (In the New Testament, "faith", "belief", and "trust" generally flow from the same word, which can be either a noun or a verb.) Faith is never blind, but depends fully on the dependability, capability, and nature of the object of faith. Faith has no power in itself; its effect flows from the power and nature of the object of faith.

Healthy leadership confidence flows from a faith in God that opens our hearts and minds to the full range of possibilities for how God might act in our leadership context. Having faith in God for leading – no matter whether the context is the Church or the marketplace – awakens us to the surprises of God's providence in our lives and the potential for God to work in any situation to bring about beneficial outcomes. Faith enlivens our leadership with joy and hope.

Begin to identify unbelief in your life with this prayer:

Dear Heavenly Father,

You have warned us to take care that we do not develop an evil, unbelieving heart that would cause us to fall away from You (Hebrews 3:12ff.). You have told us to be exhorted every day by one another and Your Word, so that we will not become hardened by the deceitfulness of sin. You have challenged us to keep our eyes fixed on Jesus so that we might hold our confidence throughout our lives (Hebrews 12:1ff.). Although I have been saved by grace through faith in Jesus Christ, faith that You have given me, I have not always applied that faith to my daily life. Although I am a believer, I have often lived practically as an

unbeliever. Although I am a Christian leader, I have often led without reference to You. Please reveal to my mind all the ways that unbelief has infected my life, so that I might repent. In Jesus' name. Amen.

Some common manifestations of unbelief:

Prayerlessness

- ❑ I do not take time every day to read the Bible and pray.
- ❑ I do not pray as much every day as God would like me to pray.
- ❑ When I encounter someone who is unwell, praying for them is not the first thing that comes to my mind or my first response.
- ❑ I do not intercede for others daily.
- ❑ I often forget to pray for someone when I said I would pray for them.
- ❑ I do not regularly pray for people to become Christians.
- ❑ When I say "grace" for a meal, I often find myself praying longer than I should.
- ❑ I do not regularly pray for those I am leading.
- ❑ I do not always pray before making key leadership decisions.
- ❑ I do not regularly pray for God to fulfil His vision for my life, ministry, work, or leadership.
- ❑ I do not ask others to pray for me as a leader.
- ❑ I do not have a sense of God's vision for my life, ministry, work, or leadership.
- ❑ Other ways that God may reveal prayerlessness to you:

Four or more ticked areas above suggests that prayerlessness is an issue.

Busyness And Hurry

- ❑ I often feel stressed because I have too many things to do.
- ❑ I often find myself walking or driving faster than I should.
- ❑ People often feel stressed and hurried when they are around me.
- ❑ People often feel that I am too busy for them.
- ❑ I get a sense of personal satisfaction from how busy I am.
- ❑ If I were not so busy, I am not sure what I would do with myself.

- ❑ I often discover that I have scheduled too many appointments in a day.
- ❑ I struggle to say "no" to new commitments and responsibilities, especially if they look really good to me.
- ❑ I do not have time to do little things for the people closest to me.
- ❑ I repeatedly fail to keep my promises and commitments to myself and others.
- ❑ I often find myself trying to make things happen.
- ❑ I often feel frustrated and irritable, especially when I think of all I need to do.
- ❑ I rarely come away from my busy life to pray and seek God.
- ❑ Other ways that God may reveal busyness and hurry to you:

Four or more ticked items above suggests that busyness and hurry are issues.

Failure To Rest

- ❑ I have difficulty slowing down.
- ❑ I often do not have or take a day off every week.
- ❑ I do not practise some kind of "Sabbath".
- ❑ I do not always take all my holidays, or I tend to take them only a few days at a time.
- ❑ I tend to stay up too late.
- ❑ I generally do not get as much sleep as I should.
- ❑ I do not have much that I enjoy doing outside of my work or ministry.
- ❑ I do not have enough time for the people who are closest to me.
- ❑ Other ways that God may reveal your failure to rest to you:

Three or more ticked items above suggests that failure to rest is an issue.

Putting One's Ministry Or Work Before Relationship With God (Idolatry)

- ❑ Although I hate to admit it, I often find myself spending so much time on ministry or work that I do not have enough time to pray, worship, and read the Bible.
- ❑ People sometimes tell me that they feel I put my ministry or work before them.
- ❑ I spend so much time doing ministry that I find it difficult to receive ministry.
- ❑ If someone examined my life, especially how I spend my time, they might struggle to see that my priorities were God first and family second.
- ❑ I often feel irritated by those who want to spend time with me, especially those close to me.
- ❑ I often feel condemned or guilty because I have not spent time with God.
- ❑ Other ways that God may reveal about how you put things before Him:

Three or more ticked items above suggests that you may be putting your ministry or work before relationship with God.

Other Manifestations Of Unbelief:

- ❑ I have trouble accepting that what God says in the Bible is true, especially for me.
- ❑ If I ordered my life according to the Bible, I would struggle to survive in this world.
- ❑ It is easier for me to apply the Bible to my personal life than my professional life.
- ❑ I often feel that the Bible may work for others but it doesn't work for me.
- ❑ I often think that God will not use me because I don't pray enough, don't know the Bible well enough, am not holy enough, or (list the reason).

- ☐ Other people's spiritual gifts, skills, or talents are more important for advancing God's kingdom than mine are.
- ☐ I do not generally sense that my leadership, ministry, or work really make any difference for God and others.
- ☐ Because of my past sins and mistakes, God will not use me like He uses other people.
- ☐ Other ways that God may reveal unbelief to you:

If you ticked any of the items above, it may suggest that unbelief is an issue. Turn away from unbelief using this prayer:

Dear Heavenly Father, Because of unbelief, Your Son Jesus could do no mighty works in Nazareth. Because of my unbelief, I have not often seen Your Son Jesus do mighty works in my life, work, ministry, and leadership. I have not always chosen the way of faith, but I have often hardened my heart and closed my mind to the truth of Your Word. I confess that my unbelief is sin. I confess the specific ways that unbelief has manifested in my life: _____ (list them).

Thank You that in Jesus Christ I am forgiven. I renounce all the ways unbelief has shown itself in my life as sin. Wash me clean of unbelief. I choose to renew my mind in the truth of who You are and in the truth of Your Word.

By faith I believe that You have cleansed my heart. I receive my place among those sanctified by faith. I choose to live by faith. I thank You that I am justified by faith and redeemed by faith. I choose to walk by faith and not by sight. I choose to exercise my leadership, do my work, and serve in ministry all by faith. By faith, I choose to receive and exercise the stewardship that You have given me. By faith I choose to obey You. By faith I choose to live my life as You decide.

I thank You for the faith You have given me, knowing that even if I have faith as small as a mustard seed, I will see the mountains move and the glory of the Lord revealed in my life. Thank You, most of all, that I have been saved by Your grace through faith, faith which You have given me through Your Son Jesus Christ in the power of Your Holy Spirit. Amen.

(Acts 15:9; Acts 26:18; Romans 1:17; Romans 3:23ff.; 2 Corinthians 5:7; Galatians 2:20; 1 Timothy 1:4; Hebrews 11; Ephesians 2:8)

Declaration Of Faith

Conclude these Steps with this declaration of faith:

I here and now, in the name of the one Lord Jesus Christ, declare my faith in the living God. I declare that there is only one God who exists as the Father, Son, and Holy Spirit. He is the creator and sustainer of all things.

I declare that Jesus Christ is the Messiah, the Word who became flesh and dwelt among us. I declare that Jesus died on the cross for the forgiveness of sins and rose bodily from the dead on the third day. I declare that He came to destroy the works of the devil, and that He has disarmed the rulers and authorities and made a public display of them, having triumphed over them by the cross.

I declare that the Holy Spirit, who lives in me, is fully God, who by His indwelling presence causes people to be born again into the Kingdom of God. The Holy Spirit seals God's people until the day of redemption. By His empowering presence, the Holy Spirit enables people to live for God and extend God's loving rulership into the whole world.

I declare that I have been saved by grace through faith in Jesus Christ, and not as a result of any works on my part. I declare that God has delivered me from the dominion of darkness and transferred me to His Kingdom. I declare that I am now seated with Christ in the heavenly places as a fully adopted child of God.

I declare that apart from Christ I can do nothing, but I can do all things through Christ who strengthens me. So I declare my complete dependence on Jesus Christ. I declare to the spiritual realms that Jesus is my only Lord and Saviour.

I declare that the Bible is trustworthy and true, the only reliable standard for faith and life. I declare that the promises God makes in the Bible are dependable and the revelation of God in the Bible is faithful.

I declare that I belong to Christ for I was bought with a price. I declare my entire being to be a living sacrifice, holy and acceptable to God through Jesus. I declare that my life and my leadership, my work and my ministry, all belong to the Lord Jesus Christ and I submit them freely to Him. I declare that Christ is in me, the hope of glory.

I declare by faith that I receive the Holy Spirit as the Father has promised. I declare by faith that I will do the works that Jesus did to the glory of the Father. I declare that I will live by faith and not by sight, seeking to please and honour God in all I say and do, to the glory of Jesus Christ.

I fully commit myself to the leadership to which God has called me: _____ (name or describe that leadership). I fully commit myself to loving and serving the people to whom God has called me. I fully commit myself to humble leadership within the sphere God has given me. I fully commit myself to bringing glory and honour to Jesus Christ through my leadership.

I declare that the Lord Jesus has all authority in heaven and on earth. I declare that Jesus Christ is coming soon. Jesus is the Alpha and the Omega, the beginning and the end. I declare that by His blood Jesus ransomed people for God from every tribe and language and people and nation, and He has made them a kingdom and priests to our God, and we shall reign on the earth.

I declare that holy, holy, holy is the Lord God Almighty, who was and is and is to come. I declare that worthy is the Lamb who was slain to receive power and wealth and wisdom and might and honour and glory and blessing. Amen!

(See Exodus 20:2, 3; Colossians 1:16, 17; John 1:1, 14; Colossians 2:15; 1 John 3:8; John 3:1ff.; Ephesians 1:13; Acts 1:8; Colossians 1:13, 14; Galatians 4:5–7; John 15:5–8; Philippians 4:13; 2 Timothy 3:15–17; 1 Corinthians 6:20; Romans 12:1; Luke 11:13; John 14:12; 2 Corinthians 5:7; Matthew 28:18; Revelation 22:12–13; Revelation 5:9–12.)

Next Steps – Changing Faulty Beliefs

We are transformed through the renewing of our minds. Before you finish the process, ask God to highlight for you where you need to change your belief system. What faulty beliefs has He helped you identify as you have gone through *The Steps To Freedom For Leaders*? Where do you need to do some work to renew your mind?

Pray the following prayer:

Heavenly Father,

I commit myself to living according to the truth. Thank you for revealing to me ways in which I have not been doing that. I ask you now through the Spirit of Truth to show me the key strongholds in my mind, the areas where my belief system has been faulty. I commit myself to renewing my mind so that I will be transformed and will become the person and the leader you want me to be.

In Jesus' name. Amen.

Sit in silence and write down areas where you realize your thinking has been faulty (i.e. does not line up with what God says in His Word). There is space for this on pages 190–191. Bear in mind that the faulty thinking will still *feel* true to you. It might help to look back through the Steps and the notes you have made in *Freed To Lead*.

Then pick no more than three key areas that you will commit to focus on to renew your mind and write them on pages 188–189. On the left-hand side write down the faulty belief and on the right side write what God says in His Word. Write as many verses as you can find that say what is really true.

For the first area, write a stronghold-buster along the following lines:

I renounce the lie that....

I announce the truth that.... [list the truth from the verses you found]

Declare it every day for the next 40 days or until you know that your belief system has changed. Then come back and do the same for the second one and then the third one. Imagine how much more effective you could be as a leader if you could deal completely with these issues. And you can!

Faulty Thinking (Lies) | **What God Says (Truth)**

Faulty Thinking (Lies)

What God Says (Truth)

Notes

Leading A *Freed To Lead* Course

LEADER'S NOTES

What Is *Freed To Lead*?

Here is a brief overview of *Freed To Lead*:

- It is a small-group discipleship course that helps people understand key Biblical principles about leadership.

- It is aimed at:
    - any Christian in a leadership position of any kind in any sphere.
    - any Christian who thinks they might be called to leadership in the future.

- It contains 10 sessions plus a ministry component called *The Steps To Freedom For Leaders*.

- It can be run in weekly sessions or all in one go as a retreat (see pages 206–209).

- The main teaching is delivered using recorded video presented by Rod Woods and Steve Goss but much of the learning takes place in facilitated discussions in small groups.

- It works equally well in a church or a workplace context.

- Participants will benefit from having first been through one of Freedom In Christ's core discipleship courses such as *The Freedom In Christ Course* or *The Grace Course* but that is not essential. *Freed To Lead* stands alone.

- An accompanying book, *Freed To Lead* by Rod Woods, provides greater depth and insight for those who would appreciate that.

- Course leaders and participants are encouraged to engage in discussion with others using the "Freed To Lead" special interest group on LinkedIn.

How Can The Course Be Used?

Freed To Lead is flexible enough to use in a variety of situations:

In Churches

Because the course is aimed at anyone in any kind of leadership as well
as anyone who feels they may be called into leadership, it is likely to be
of interest to the majority of people in a typical church. It can, therefore,
run as a 10-week discipleship course (plus ministry component). It works
particularly well as a follow-on to *The Freedom In Christ Discipleship
Course* or *The Grace Course*.

In The Workplace

The subject matter of *Freed To Lead* lends itself extremely well to groups
meeting in a workplace context. The main teaching element in each session
is around 30 minutes which allows it to run comfortably in a lunch break.
In this scenario we would advise taking two weeks per session: the first to
receive the teaching and the second to discuss it.

In Small Groups

In our experience, the most effective way to deliver the material is in small
groups with plenty of time for interaction and discussion. If people miss
a session, try to ensure that they have access to the DVD so that they can
catch up.

In Larger Meetings

It is also possible to use the course in a larger meeting such as a Sunday
service or a mid-week setting where there are no established small groups.
You would bring everyone together to watch the main teaching and divide
them into groups for discussion.

What Are The Course Components?

Freed To Lead Leader's Guide
ISBN: 978 0 85721 706 6

We recommend that, if possible, everyone leading a group has their own copy of this Leader's Guide which also incorporates the content of the Participant's Guide (below). It contains essential information on leading the course, particularly on leading the Pause For Thought discussions. Note that, although it includes a precis of the teaching for each session, it does not include the entire script as the main teaching is designed to be delivered using the DVDs.

Freed To Lead DVD Set
PAL version ISBN: 978 0 85721 711 0
NTSC version ISBN: 978 0 85721 747 9

Contains the main teaching for each of the ten sessions plus *The Steps To Freedom For Leaders*. The DVDs pause automatically for the Pause For Thought discussion times and for the prayer times during the Steps. Press play to continue when your group is ready. The DVD has optional subtitles in English for those who are hearing-impaired or whose mother tongue is not English. Available in PAL and NTSC formats.

Freed To Lead Participant's Guide
ISBN: 978 0 85721 708 0

Each participant will need a copy of the Participant's Guide which contains comprehensive notes for each session and the Pause For Thought questions as well as *The Steps To Freedom For Leaders*. As well as enabling participants to follow the teaching, the notes contain additional information.

Freed To Lead Book
ISBN: 978 0 85721 704 2

The accompanying book by Rod Woods is recommended for anyone involved in leading a course as it goes into topics in greater depth and covers even more ground than the course itself. It is also recommended for participants who want to explore the content in more detail.

What Is In Each Session?

Each of the ten teaching sessions is structured in the same way and contains several common components.

Welcome

Each session begins with "Welcome", which is an open question for discussion. It is designed simply to stimulate discussion and openness in your group. Larger groups, or groups who do not know one another well, would especially benefit from the "Welcome" time. These questions are best discussed as people are settling down with a cup of coffee or tea – and perhaps some good pastry – and getting ready for the session. Take care not to allow this time to run for too long.

Worship

Each session continues with "Worship". We encourage you to have a worship component for each one of your meetings. Worship centres our lives on God through Jesus Christ and welcomes the Holy Spirit to protect and lead the sessions of the course. Because of the diversity throughout the Church, we do not prescribe a particular means or form of worship but simply encourage you to allow the Holy Spirit to lead you.

If you are doing the course as a weekend retreat, then you might arrange worship at various times during the retreat, such as the beginning, the end and after meal breaks. We would encourage you to structure these times of worship according to the normal customs and practices of your group or ministry. Where possible, we would encourage both times of singing and praying for one another in your worship during your retreat.

If you are doing the course on a weekly basis, we would suggest having a time of worship during each session. This time of worship could be as simple as singing a song together *a capella* or as complex as you like. Feel free to determine the content and length of this worship based on the needs of your group, the style of your ministry or the projected time that you have available.

To assist you in developing the worship component, we have provided a worship focus for each session based on Psalm 37. During the time of difficulty I (Rod) describe in session 1, I found Psalm 37 to be a great encouragement. It seemed to speak directly into our situation and encourage us with the mercy and grace of God.

For the first session, we use the entirety of Psalm 37. In the remaining sessions, we have divided Psalm 37 into ten parts. There are several ways that you might choose to develop worship around these passages of Psalm 37. You might choose one or two worship songs used by your ministry that seem to reflect the truths of the psalm. You might spend time thanking and praising God for the aspects of His character revealed by the psalm. You might also spend time thanking God for any promises contained in the passage. We give suggestions for each passage, but we encourage you to have freedom in this.

Word

The main teaching in *Freed To Lead* (see the "Watch" section below) is based on the Bible as God's Word, but is not intended as a Bible study. We have, therefore, provided a "Word" component for groups that might like to study the Bible more directly. It provides a study of a Bible passage that can aid our understanding of leadership and anchor each session more deeply in biblical truth.

The "Word" component is optional but might especially benefit a church that decides to offer the course to the entire congregation. If you use the "Word" component, we would encourage you to allow at least 30 minutes for it. You will, of course, need to ensure that you leave enough time (and energy!) in your meeting to do the "Watch" component, which provides the central teaching for the course.

An alternative use of the "Word" component is for small group Bible study or individual Bible study as "homework" in between the sessions of the course. Participants can then work through the Bible study questions at their own pace.

A further possibility is to lift the "Word" component from the context of the course and use it as a follow-up Bible study in small groups. This would allow people and groups to review some of the teaching again as they discuss how the Bible shapes their leadership.

Watch

The "Watch" component of each session with its integrated Pause For Thought questions, forms the heart of the *Freed To Lead* teaching content.

Participants will watch the teaching on the *Freed To Lead* DVDs which pause automatically for two Pause For Thought discussion times per session. Each "Watch" component is approximately 30 minutes in length (excluding discussion times).

Much of the learning will take place in the two Pause For Thought discussions where people will break into small groups to discuss the teaching.

You will need to plan at least 45–60 minutes of each session for the "Watch" component.

This Leader's Guide contains some important background information, including some excerpts from the talks, so that you can ensure your people get the most out of the material. Some of the material will be new to people, so your group may need to re-watch certain parts of the teaching or take more time going through it, pausing when there is anything people struggle to understand fully.

Towards the end of each session, we give a "leadership dilemma". These are issues leaders face that have no easy solution. We recommend you read the section on "Understanding The Difference Between Problems And Dilemmas" before beginning your course so that you can help participants realize that dilemmas cannot be solved, only managed.

Walk It Out

Each session concludes with a "Walk It Out" component. This component has four purposes.

First, we hope that people will determine one practical thing that they can do to implement what they have learned into their leadership.

Second, after the first session, we provide opportunity for people to debrief the previous session and share how they have done with their commitment from the previous session.

Third, we give people an opportunity to review and reflect on their own leadership journey. Often these can be times of significant personal discovery.

Finally, and most importantly, we want people to pray for one another, particularly regarding their leadership. Each session has a slightly different focus for prayer, often connected to the material for that session. This prayer time might become one of the most important parts of your meeting.

How Does The Ministry Component Work?

The Steps To Freedom For Leaders on pages 133–192 is a resource focused on the personal and spiritual issues common to people in leadership, be it leadership in the marketplace, leadership in the church, or leadership in the home and community.

It is designed to be used once participants have completed the ten teaching sessions and is a **vital** part of *Freed To Lead*. We would encourage you to do everything you can to ensure that participants engage in the process.

If your group is small enough for you to arrange for everyone to be led personally through the process with a prayer partner in attendance, that will be the most effective route.

However, most will choose for logistical reasons to take everyone through at once on an away day (or as part of a *Freed To Lead* retreat). In this context, participants will say some prayers out loud together and will then spread out to "do business" with God on their own. It is helpful for them to have leaders they can call on at any point to answer questions or help them through any parts they find particularly difficult.

The process is self-explanatory and the DVD will guide you through.

You will find further information by reading the introduction to the process on pages 134–136 and in the leader's notes for the session.

We would strongly suggest that you go through the process yourself before you take others through.

How Can I Make The Course As Effective As Possible?

Our top tips for course leaders:

- Determine the optimum session length for your group (see pages 204–205). Each session could take as little as one hour or as long as two hours, depending on the needs and preferences of your group. We suggest that for best results you allow at least 90 minutes for each session.
- Include the Bible studies in the "Word" section if you possibly can. Alternatively, encourage your participants to do the Bible studies on their own or with a friend in between sessions, ideally before the corresponding session.
- Encourage full participation in all discussions. Make sure that everyone has an opportunity to share, even those who might seem reluctant. Remember that much of the learning people will experience will come from the discussion times.
- In order to benefit most from the course, we would encourage participants to have been through *The Freedom In Christ Discipleship Course* or *The Grace Course* before participating in this course and also *The Steps To Freedom In Christ*. This is not essential, but we have found that people will get even more out of *Freed To Lead* if they have done so.
- Read *Freed To Lead* by Rod Woods, ideally before you lead the course. Although not essential, it will give you much more detail and some valuable insights into the material. In addition, the book covers many topics not included in the course that may be valuable to your course participants.
- Determine the date and venue for your away day to do *The Steps To Freedom For Leaders* before you begin your course and ensure participants have it in their diaries. Emphasize that this is an integral part of the course and not to be missed!

Helping Participants Engage

The more participants engage with *Freed To Lead*, the more they will get out of it. There are two elements in the Participant's Guide that are designed to help with this.

"Your Leadership Journey"

Throughout *Freed To Lead* participants are encouraged to create a timeline of their leadership experiences. It is designed to help them look back at their past leadership experiences – both positive and negative – in order to gain insights and work out how to apply what they learn to their present leadership context. It is on pages 17 and 18. It works best if participants use separate sheets of paper for this as the space in the Participant's Guide is limited.

Participants are referred specifically to the timeline in the "Walk It Out" sections of the first three sessions and again in Session 7. However, it would be beneficial to point them to the timeline more frequently than that.

"Faulty Thinking Versus What God Says" Sheets

Paul says in Romans 12:2 that transformation comes through renewing the mind. The first step towards doing that is to become aware of areas where our thinking is faulty, that is where it does not line up completely with what God says in His Word.

When participants become aware of any faulty thinking, they are encouraged to write it on pages 188–189 of the Participant's Guide together with verses from the Bible that state what is really true.

They will then be able to go on to renew their mind using the "stronghold-busting" process (see page 187). Participants who take the trouble to do this will make significant steps forward.

You are encouraged to refer your group to these pages at the end of every session so that they can record any faulty thinking that has come to light.

How Long Should I Allow Per Session?

Assuming you are planning a session per week, this section will help you determine the optimum time to allow.

Here are a suggested range of timings for each component:

Welcome	5–10 minutes
Worship	5–15 minutes
Word	30–45 minutes
Watch	45–60 minutes
Walk It Out	10–20 minutes

You will note that if you used the maximum time for each component, your session would last 150 minutes which would be too long for most groups since many people are likely to lose focus. We suggest that you plan your sessions to last no more than 120 minutes and, in our experience, 90 minutes is usually the optimum.

Groups who do not have the luxury of time or who want to focus just on the core *Freed To Lead* teaching, especially groups such as leadership teams who know one another well, are advised to spend almost all of their time on "Watch" and "Walk It Out". They could complete a session in as little as 60 minutes.

It is especially important to keep a careful eye on how long "Welcome" and "Worship" each takes, because these are areas where most groups overrun consistently. "Walk It Out" is very important, so it is better to plan a shorter time for the opening components so that you do not take time away from the end.

The teaching sessions are all around 30 minutes in length but there is some variation – see the following page.

Detailed Timings For The DVD

Each teaching session on the DVD contains two Pause For Thought discussion times and the DVD will pause automatically with the questions on the screen (they are also in the Participant's Guide). Detailed timings for each DVD are shown below. Pause For Thought discussion times appear between each part.

Session 1	Session 2
Part 1: 8' 45"	Part 1: 3' 18"
Part 2: 9' 03"	Part 2: 28' 18"
Part 3: 5' 00"	Part 3: 1' 34"
Session 3	**Session 4**
Part 1: 4' 12"	Part 1: 2' 51"
Part 2: 24' 41"	Part 2: 22' 41"
Part 3: 1' 37"	Part 3: 0' 56"
Session 5	**Session 6**
Part 1: 2' 31"	Part 1: 21' 46"
Part 2: 23' 31"	Part 2: 7' 28"
Part 3: 1' 29"	Part 3: 2' 13"
Session 7	**Session 8**
Part 1: 12' 36"	Part 1: 2' 02"
Part 2: 15' 11"	Part 2: 26' 23"
	Part 3: 2' 02"
Session 9	**Session 10**
Part 1: 3' 44"	Part 1: 13' 21"
Part 2: 26' 22"	Part 2: 12' 29"
Part 3: 1' 02"	Part 3: 1' 13"
Steps To Freedom For Leaders	
Introduction: 6' 33"	Step 5: 7' 02"
Step 1: 11' 52"	Step 6: 9' 40"
Step 2: 6' 35"	Step 7: 22' 54"
Step 3: 4' 11"	Conclusion: 12' 10"
Step 4: 5' 08"	(Timings exclude the time needed for personal prayer.)

Freed To Lead As A Retreat

When we first developed *Freed To Lead*, we offered it as a retreat for leaders. We envisioned that leaders would have a time away with the Lord not only to process the teaching and to work their way through *The Steps To Freedom For Leaders* but also to have some time away with God so that they might seek God's will for their future leadership and receive fresh vision from God, not only for their leadership but also for their people-system.

As we tried various permutations of the schedule, we discovered that, in order to provide a reasonably beneficial retreat, it is necessary to allow at least three full days. We suspect that this will be the case for any group desiring to do *Freed To Lead* as a retreat. We also discovered that an ideal retreat would last at least four days, but most leaders would likely not commit a full four days to the process.

We have developed the following retreat schedules with these details in mind. If you decide to offer the course as a retreat it is important to remember that it will be a very intense time. Some group members feel like they are drinking from a fire hydrant! So you will need to manage the time and energy of your group very carefully in order to benefit the most from the retreat.

An ideal scenario for those deciding to offer the course as a retreat might be to offer the teaching on one weekend and then hold a separate day away the next weekend. If you decide to use this option then you should find the schedule easy to amend accordingly.

We have provided two versions of the schedule, both of which are highly adaptable. The first version of the schedule inserts the Steps at various points within the three days. The second version has the Steps as the last day of the retreat. In both versions, groups will normally not do the "Welcome", "Worship", "Word", and "Walk It Out" parts of each session, but these activities can be inserted throughout the retreat as desired.

Freed To Lead Retreat Timing 1:
Day One

10.00–10.30	Arrival and Fellowship
10.30–10.45	Worship
10.45–11.45	Session 1 – The Adventure of Leadership
11.45–12.00	Break
12.00–13.00	Session 2 – Real Christian Leadership
13.00–14.00	Lunch
14.00–14.15	Worship
14.15–15.15	Session 3 – Being And Doing
15.15–15.45	Break
15.45–16.45	Session 4 – Leading In Your Context
16.45–17.00	Break
17.00–18.00	Steps To Freedom For Leaders – Steps One and Two
18.30–19.30	Dinner
19.45–21.00	Worship; Session 5 – Building Healthy People-Systems
	Prayer for one another in small groups

Day Two

08.00	Breakfast
09.15–09.30	Worship
09.30–10.30	Session 6 – Overcoming Personal Anxiety
10.30–11.00	Break
11.00–12.00	Session 7 – Overcoming Group Anxiety
12.00–12.45	Praying for our personal leadership contexts in small groups
13.00–14.00	Lunch
14.00–14.15	Worship
14.15–18.30	Steps To Freedom For Leaders – Steps Three, Four, and Five
18.30–19.30	Dinner
19.45–21.00	Worship; Session 8 – Building And Keeping Trust

Day Three

08.00	Breakfast
09.15–09.30	Worship
09.30–10.30	Session 9 – Overcoming Personal Pitfalls
10.30–11.00	Break
11.00–12.00	Session 10 – Overcoming Group Pitfalls
12.00–12.45	Steps To Freedom For Leaders – Step Six
13.00–14.00	Lunch
14.00–14.15	Worship
14.15–15.00	Praying for one another and our leadership challenges
15.00–15.30	Break
15.30–16.15	Steps To Freedom For Leaders – Step Seven
16.15–17.00	Closing worship and closing prayers for one another

Freed To Lead Retreat Timing 2:
Day One

10.00–10.30	Arrival and fellowship
10.30–10.45	Worship
10.45–11.45	Session 1 – The Adventure Of Leadership
11.45–12.00	Break
12.00–13.00	Session 2 – Real Christian Leadership
13.00–14.00	Lunch
14.00–14.15	Worship
14.15–15.15	Session 3 – Being And Doing
15.15–15.45	Break
15.45–16.45	Session 4 – Leading In Your Context
16.45–18.00	Free Time (or buffer time if you want to start the retreat later)
18.30–19.30	Dinner
19.45–21.00	Worship; Session 5 – Building Healthy People-Systems Prayer for one another in small groups

Day Two

08.00	Breakfast
09.15–09.30	Worship
09.30–10.30	Session 6 – Overcoming Personal Anxiety
10.30–11.00	Break
11.00–12.00	Session 7 – Overcoming Group Anxiety
12.00–12.45	Praying for our personal leadership contexts in small groups
13.00–14.00	Lunch
14.00–14.15	Worship
14.15–15.15	Session 8 – Building And Keeping Trust
15.15–15.30	Break
15.30–16.30	Session 9 – Overcoming Personal Pitfalls
16.30–18.00	Free Time (or buffer time as needed)
18.30–19.30	Dinner
19.45–21.00	Worship; Session 10 – Overcoming Group Pitfalls

Day Three

Follow one of the proposed schedules for the away day.

What Is The Best Way To Prepare Myself To Lead?

Go Through The Teaching In The Course For Yourself

The very best way of preparing yourself to lead the course is to go through it for yourself. You may be able to sit in on a course at another church or you could simply watch the DVDs. Reading the accompanying book is another excellent way of getting hold of the teaching before leading the course.

Have A Personal *Steps To Freedom In Christ* Appointment

A critical part of your own preparation is to experience *The Steps To Freedom In Christ* for yourself. It sends a powerful message to participants that "this is for everyone" when the leader says, "I did it and I benefitted from it." Ideally, this is something that you will go through in your own church, but, if that is not possible, Freedom In Christ can often put leaders in touch with a local church that will be happy to serve them in this way, provided that it is with a view to getting started in their own church.

Work Out And Use A "Stronghold-Buster"

"Stronghold-Busting" is a strategy to renew your mind recommended in *Freed To Lead.* If you are able to speak from personal experience about how you have used it in your own life, the impact on participants will be that much greater.

Register With Freedom In Christ

The objective of Freedom In Christ Ministries is to equip Christian leaders to help their people live in freedom and grow in Christ. If you are a leader, we recommend that you register with us as a user of this course. You will receive news, hints and tips, and access to a special section of our website. Registering is free of charge and can be done at www.ficm.org.uk/register.

Getting The Most Out Of The Course

LEADER'S NOTES

Getting The Most From Group Discussions

In each session we will ask course participants to form small groups in order to work through the Pause For Thought questions.

If your group is larger than eight, split people down into sub-groups of no more than seven or eight for the discussions and mix the groups up each week. For variety, consider some discussions in smaller groups of three to four to allow quieter ones to talk.

As a leader of a discussion group, one of your main roles is to try to get others to talk. Don't be afraid of silences.

In addition to the questions given, you could start any Pause For Thought with the following open questions:

- What do you think about what you have just heard?
- Was there anything you heard that you didn't understand or that needs further clarification?
- How do you think what you have heard applies to you?

Try not to let the conversation wander too far from the main points and keep an eye on the time.

Draw the discussion to a close at the appropriate time by summarizing briefly. The Pause For Thought objectives in this Leader's Guide make a good basis for that summary.

In order to get the most from your groups, it is helpful to ensure that course participants are given the following guidelines:

1. If leaders have not been assigned, each group should begin by choosing one person to be the leader. The leader is responsible for:
    - keeping the group focused on the material and not allowing the group to become distracted by peripheral issues or casual conversation;

- making sure that the group works through the material within the time allotted;
- encouraging every person in the group to participate, especially by directly asking people to share their insights with the group.

2. One person must not do all the talking or sharing in your group. If the leader perceives that someone is contributing too much, the leader should ask the person to wait until others have had a chance to share. Group members are responsible to make sure that the leader does not monopolize the group time.

3. Every group member is responsible to participate in the group work. Remember that your insights really are valuable to others.

4. Ask questions. Develop a sense of curiosity. Bring any questions you cannot answer to the course leader for discussion.

5. Stay on task. It is easy to get side-tracked by trivial issues or issues that do not relate directly to the material at hand. Save the discussion of these issues for afterwards.

6. If you sense a discussion might be potentially sensitive, ask people to form groups with people of the same gender. Some people feel more comfortable discussing personal issues with people of the same gender.

7. When possible, try to get in a group with someone you do not know well. Small group work provides a great opportunity for people to get to know each other and develop lasting friendships.

8. Maintain confidentiality. Sometimes people will share personal details in the course of discussion. These details should not be shared outside the group without the person's explicit permission.

Troubleshooting In Group Discussions

Occasionally, you may have some difficulties with the people who are in the course. Course leaders should approach such difficulties calmly and prayerfully. Below, we have listed some of the more common issues along with some suggestions about how to deal effectively with these issues.

1. Monopolizing time and process: One or more people tend to talk too much or take too long to share.
    *   Gently interrupt and ask a relevant, short-answer question that changes the flow of thought. Then ask another person to share or say something like, "This is good sharing, but we need to move on for the sake of time."
    *   Begin the question by asking others to share before you ask the one who tends to monopolize the time.
    *   Speak with the person outside the meeting and encourage them to wait until others have shared before they share.
    *   People who monopolize the time usually have other issues.

2. Uncommunicativeness: One or more people do not talk much.
    *   Specifically ask individual people to respond, and wait for their response.
    *   Do not rush people. Give people time to think.
    *   Let silence work for you.
    *   Reassure people that they do not have to respond.

3. Non-attendance: One or more people fail to come to the meetings, or continually arrive late.
    *   Phone or email people individually and encourage them to attend.
    *   Find out whether there are specific reasons for a person's nonattendance, and offer to help them troubleshoot.
    *   Remind people how important the process is as well as their regular participation in the process.

4. Tangential issues: People want to discuss issues that may be important but are not the focus of the course discussions.

- Remind people of the limited time and encourage them to stay on task.
- Politely interrupt a tangential conversation and encourage people to resume the conversation after the course meeting.
- Listen for the Holy Spirit. Occasionally, a seemingly tangential conversation needs to become the real focus for the meeting.

5. Breaking confidentiality: people gossip or share inappropriately outside the course meeting.
   - Interrupt the inappropriate sharing (inside or outside the meeting) with a reminder of the need for confidentiality.
   - Remind your group of the need for confidentiality.
   - In severe cases, consult with the pastor.

6. Serious personal issues: people begin to share personal issues that are beyond your or the group's ability to counsel (even though the issue may be related to the topic) in the context of the course meeting.
   - Reassure the person of your care and concern, but gently explain that the issue is beyond what you can deal with in this context.
   - Encourage the person to set up a personal *Steps To Freedom In Christ* appointment to help resolve the issue.
   - Ask permission to speak with the pastor about the issue on the person's behalf in order to seek further counsel.
   - Offer to meet with the person (when appropriate) over coffee to discuss the matter more fully.
   - Encourage the person to set up an appointment with the pastor in order to discuss the issue.

7. Manifestations: people report spiritual interference with their participation; people respond to an issue with intense anger, bitterness, resentment, or sorrow; people report consistent problems reading the Bible, praying, or completing the work (other than simply running out of time).
   - Stop and pray for the person immediately.
   - Reassure the person of your caring and concern for them, and

remind them that this is a safe place and it is acceptable to express such strong emotion.

- Strongly encourage the person to go through *The Steps To Freedom in Christ*.
- Encourage the person to meet with the pastor as soon as possible.
- Report what happened to the pastor for consultation.

8. Time Issues: people continually report having too little time.
   - Make sure that the group is not using their time ineffectively.
   - Encourage people to complete as much as possible in the time they have allotted and then not worry about the rest.
   - Help people think creatively about their time.

Understanding The Difference Between Problems And Dilemmas

Throughout the course, we talk about leadership "dilemmas" – there is one in each session. We have found that many leaders do not fully understand the concept of dilemmas. This brief article (adapted from the book, *Freed To Lead*) will help you understand the difference between a problem and a dilemma. Understanding the difference will help leaders think more creatively about the situations they face. It will also help leaders avoid a lot of problems they create by mistaking dilemmas for problems.

As leaders, we face many things every day that we consider to be problems. Many of these things we consider as problems are actually dilemmas.

Problems are issues that can be solved and resolved. Problems have solutions. Normally, we can think through problems in order to achieve a satisfactory resolution. Problems may often respond to the application of technology, such as various computer programs.

For example, "2+2 = 4" is a common mathematical problem. It has a solution. If someone gets into debt, then there are numerous solutions to get them out of debt. They can change their spending habits. They can live within their means according to a budget. If someone drives into our car and dents it, we can take the car to the body shop and have it repaired. If we want to drive from London to New York City, we can look on a map and discover that we will have a problem with the Atlantic Ocean. Although the solution might be challenging, we can find a solution to this problem. That is the nature of problems – they have solutions.

Dilemmas are issues that by their nature resist solutions. We have no easy way to resolve them. Normally, we can only manage them while we work our way through them. Dilemmas often require a lot of time as well as a thoughtful response from leaders to work themselves out. Occasionally, the best we can do is learn to live with the dilemma and not allow it to undermine our people-system or our leadership.

For example, climate change is a dilemma. It has no quick fixes. It will require the co-operation of many people and nations who normally would not co-operate with one another to begin to resolve climate change. Even scientists themselves debate how to resolve this complex issue, with some scientists questioning whether there is even an issue called "climate change".

A husband and wife who are having struggles relating to one another well are facing a dilemma. We might try to identify certain behaviours of the husband or the wife as problems, but when we understand the complex nature of human relationships we quickly realize that these so-called "problems" have no easy solutions. As soon as the husband changes his behaviour in one area, the wife will often change her behaviour in another area thereby continuing the relational struggles. Bringing health to this relationship does not have straightforward answers.

A church struggling with changing demographics has a dilemma. The church cannot simply decide to adopt a new style of worship or some new technology in order to reach the newcomers in the community. Churches in these situations face a number of complex issues, including how the church is organized, the kinds of ministries the church offers, the interrelationships of the people within the church, the average tenure of people within the church, and the socioeconomic backgrounds of people in the church. We simply cannot tell these churches to do one or two things that will lead to a clear resolution of these issues.

The key is this: when we have a dilemma, by definition there are no easy answers. If you try to find a quick fix for a dilemma, it will cause additional difficulties. If we mistake a dilemma for a problem as a leader, then we will create crises and conflicts of will in our people-system. The challenge is that dilemmas and problems look very similar to one another, but they are radically different.

Let's consider a story that illustrates all this. Annie enjoyed challenging things and pushing boundaries. Because of this, she had attended many different churches in the previous ten years. In each church she had experienced the same cycle. The churches warmly welcomed her at first. Then they became annoyed at her behaviour. They tried to "solve" her behaviour with various techniques and tools. Finally, they would ask her to leave the church. Annie began to expect these cycles which encouraged her to behave in ever more challenging ways.

Few people understood Annie's background. When she was a young girl, her father had rejected her and her mother had neglected her. She learned that the only way she could get her mother's attention was to act out and misbehave. She also learned that poor behaviour would get her more attention at school. Although she knew that such behaviour damaged her relationships, she continued to behave in these ways because they saved her from the pain of rejection that she had come to expect from all her relationships.

Annie finally came to Frank's church. Frank's church embraced the principles of Freedom In Christ Ministries, seeking to create a relational culture based on our identity in Christ, forgiveness, repentance, and grace. Annie joined a course during the weekly fellowship night. From the very first evening, she challenged the course leader. The course leader remained calm, addressed some of the issues Annie raised, and then calmly continued with the course. When Annie challenged her a second time, the course leader simply asked her to hold her comments until the end so that others could have an opportunity to participate.

When Annie later complained to Frank about the course leader, Frank listened to Annie's concerns but calmly supported the course leader. Although Annie raised one or two legitimate points, Frank still supported the course leader as he spoke with Annie. He did raise the issues later in private with the course leader, who received Frank's encouragement and made the necessary corrections.

Although she tried her best to force Frank's church to reject her, they continued to show Annie grace and forgiveness. They did not try to "fix" or "solve" Annie, but neither would they allow Annie to distract them from their healthy functioning. Annie felt attracted to the health she encountered in the church. She also began to change her behaviour so that it became healthier as well. Annie remained involved in Frank's church for almost two years.

Annie's behaviour created a dilemma. Her behaviour had no easy solutions. Annie was not a problem that needed to be fixed, but a person who needed to experience love and grace. Churches who had tried to "fix" Annie and force her to conform had only driven Annie away. They had also created more turmoil and strife within the church as they sought to "fix" Annie.

Most of the situations leaders face are dilemmas, not problems. We cannot solve them; we can only look after them as they work themselves out. The challenge is that most leaders feel more confident solving problems than resolving dilemmas. We like to develop clear-cut solutions to the issues we face. We do not like the messiness of dilemmas with no clear or easy resolution. Generally, problems are easier than dilemmas, requiring less time and energy to deal with.

Leaders must remember that people are not problems to be solved. Even their so-called "problem" behaviours often have no easy solutions. Of course, in one sense, "problem" behaviours do have an easy solution – repent and stop doing them! – but the complex personalities that give rise to these behaviours cannot be "solved" in the same way. People normally create dilemmas.

At the end of each session, we give a "leadership dilemma". These are issues leaders face that have no easy solution. Many books will try to present ways to solve these dilemmas easily. However, we have discovered that most often leaders simply need to learn how to live with these dilemmas without allowing them to sidetrack them or cause anxiety in them.

Creating A Culture Of Healthy Leadership In Your Own Organisation

Our hope is that you might use this resource to help create a culture of healthy leadership in your leadership context that will raise up healthy leaders. We would advocate a three-step process to achieve this.

First, take your people through *The Freedom In Christ Discipleship Course*, including the day away for *The Steps To Freedom In Christ*. These two resources help people establish a good foundation for their identity in Christ and equip them with the basic tools to get the most out of *Freed To Lead*.

Second, take your core leadership team through *Freed To Lead*. You might do this as a weekly gathering for your team or as part of a long-weekend retreat (three full days is best). Be sure that your core leadership team works through *The Steps To Freedom For Leaders* either in pairs, as part of a day away, or as part of the weekend retreat.

Third, offer *Freed To Lead* to all the people in your leadership context. We would encourage you not simply to choose those you consider to be "leaders" to participate, but to invite everyone to go through the course. We have found that many people do not think of themselves as leaders but after going through the course discover how God has designed and called them as leaders.

Fourth, repeat the process, encouraging others in your leadership context to lead the next time through. We find that many people learn the materials more fully when they lead the course.

As you go through this process, you can involve people from across the generations. This is a resource to help grow young leaders as well as to help encourage older leaders. When possible, involve both younger and older people in the course. The mixture will help everyone grow and develop as leaders.

If you follow this process, we believe that you will create a culture of healthy leadership in your leadership context.

The purpose of this session is to present an overview of *Freed To Lead* and an introduction to the main principles of Freedom In Christ's teaching. We also hope to encourage leaders, especially those who have been struggling or who have felt like failures, by presenting some common reasons why people struggle to lead.

DISCUSSION AIMS

Pause For Thought 1 (page 12)
The goal of this Pause For Thought is to help people begin thinking about how they define leadership. One key point: around the world, people have more difficulty defining leadership than they do deciding what makes a good leader.

Pause For Thought 2 (page 15)
The goal of this Pause For Thought is to help people see that leadership is not easy, even though so many books or conferences want to make it sound easy. We hope that people will overcome their discouragement and realize they can be good leaders in spite of the difficulty.

WORSHIP

- Choose an opening song of praise.
- Read Psalm 37 out loud in your group, without comment.
- Pause for a quiet moment of reflection on the content of the Psalm.
- Pray for the course.

Notes for participants are on pages 9–16.

Purpose Of *Freed To Lead*

Around the world every culture recognizes the vital importance of leadership for the well-being of society. Most societies consider leadership, in one form or another, the noblest of aspirations and callings.

I believe leadership is a great adventure. I am excited about it and passionate about seeing other people join the adventure. God has created this adventure of leadership and invited us to share in His plan to change lives and transform the world through our leadership.

The adventure takes us places we never dreamed of going. It stretches and challenges us to the limits of our endurance. Whether our adventure seems great or small at the time, we can never fully anticipate what our leadership might accomplish in the world.

The leadership adventure engages seemingly ordinary people in seemingly ordinary roles – mother, father, supervisor, entrepreneur, boss, pastor – in processes and activities that transform lives and shape our societies. We, as leaders, may think of ourselves as small and insignificant – we may not even think of ourselves as "leaders" at all – but God uses us in ways often beyond our perception.

I **know** that you can be a great leader. And I know that a company of great Christian leaders will change the world for Jesus. But I also know that many people give up leading because it gets tough and painful. So many great leaders think they are failures, when in fact they are changing lives for the good all around them. The purpose of this course is to enable Christians to lead confidently from a vision of Christian leadership based on our identity in Christ.

The Bible And Leadership

In this course, the Bible is our foundation for understanding leadership. We believe that Jesus showed us real leadership. However, we're not going to try to reduce Jesus or the Bible to a set of principles. Knowing Jesus and the Bible involves a living relationship with God.

We're not going to limit the Bible and Jesus to private morality. We believe that Jesus and the Bible have relevance in the "real" world, even the public world of the marketplace.

We're also not going to take worldly methods and styles of leadership and give them a Christian veneer. We'll present a vision for genuinely Christian leadership. We believe that Christian leadership is the leadership the world really needs today – and not just the Church. This is one of our strongest convictions about leadership.

Leadership Is Tough

We do have a theme verse for the course. It's one of my favourite passages of the Bible, 2 Timothy 1:6–7, which we translate like this:

For this reason I remind you to fan into flame the gift of God, which is in you through the laying on of my hands, for God did not give us a spirit of cowardice but of power and love and self-control.

Leadership takes courage. God has given us what we need as Christians for courageous leadership – power, love and self-control. We need these things because leadership can be tough.

We want to give you a true picture of leadership. So many courses and books seem to suggest that leadership is easy. They imply that if you just apply their principles, their lessons, or their examples then you would surely get their results. But the real world is not that neat and tidy.

Why Is It So Difficult To Lead – Especially For Christians?

Many leaders I talk with feel like failures. They have not experienced the successes promised by the courses and the books. They seem to have constant struggles with their followers. They wrestle continually with depression and discouragement, assuming that if they were good leaders then leadership would not be so difficult for them. They have believed the lies peddled by the world.

No adventure worth having is easy. Adventures worthy of the name test our stamina and courage. We may often want to quit, but something compels us forward. This is certainly true of the leadership adventure. We often do not choose the adventure of leadership for ourselves, but people or circumstances – or God – seem to choose us instead.

If you're struggling as a leader, it doesn't mean that something is wrong with you. We see a number of things that work together to make leadership especially difficult in our times. Perhaps you can see something here in your situation that is affecting your leadership.

First, people are overwhelmed. We're overwhelmed by the pace of change, the challenges we face, and the choices we have. Overwhelmed people find it difficult to respond well to leadership. Overwhelmed leaders struggle to lead.

Second, people are overloaded. People are flooded with so much information and sensory input that they can no longer process it all. Alvin Toffler called this "information overload". People have so many choices today that they experience what's called choice overload. They get stressed and feel paralyzed so they can't make well-informed choices. Overloaded people simply don't know who to follow. Overloaded leaders become paralysed.

The third reason leaders find it so difficult to lead is that people are unfocused. This includes leaders. We all need a coherent worldview, a strong set of values, and a clear focus for our lives. Our focus helps us to say "no" to things, while letting us choose what's really important for our lives.

Because we don't have a clear focus, many things capture our attention and draw us away from how we want to live our lives. We become subject to the worldviews, values and focuses of other people and groups.

We need a worldview, values, and focus shaped by the Bible if we are to lead effectively as Christians.

Next, leadership is difficult because people are undisciplined. As the last verse of Judges says, everyone does what is right in his or her own eyes. There's a sense of lawlessness in the world today, where everything seems up for grabs. There's a rapidly changing sense of morality which rejects the historic values on which our society is built. Even leaders themselves often become undisciplined.

Fifth, people are anxious. They feel like society is broken. They're uneasy because of all the changes going on. They feel unstable, losing hope and expecting loss. Anxious people resist leadership. Anxious leaders cannot lead well.

Finally, leaders today feel disempowered and demoralized. Many simply quit and retreat. In their place many surrogate leaders arise: technocrats, autocrats, bureaucrats, plutocrats, terrorists, extremists, and subversives. When real leaders succeed people sabotage them. They refuse to follow and they withdraw from the leadership process. They want leaders to make them feel good. And when leaders tell them the truth, people undermine the leaders.

Sometimes leadership can seem so tough that it makes me wonder why anyone would want to be a leader. Leadership creates a number of dilemmas – challenges with no easy, clear-cut solutions.

In each session we will consider a "Leadership Dilemma".
A dilemma is a challenge with no straightforward solution. Please see the article "The Difference Between A Problem And A Dilemma" for background information on this.

Here is the first leadership dilemma:

Our society needs real, effective leadership. Such leadership is the only way we can resolve the great issues of our times, whether they are personal, social, economic, or global. Yet the very people who need true leadership are the ones who consciously or unconsciously undermine, attack, sabotage, and destroy leadership.

So often, it seems all we hear about are phenomenal leadership "success" stories. Stories about people becoming millionaires overnight, or churches growing to 5,000 people in one year, or companies becoming instant successes might be exciting, but they simply don't represent the real world that most of us live in.

Churches often give the picture that leaders should be "nice" and "agreeable", rather like a doting grandpa. We say that leaders should be "servants", which often means we expect them to act like our butler, looking after our every whim and meeting all our "needs". Churches often only respect marketplace leaders for the money they give and the committees they serve on. This picture of leadership looks weak and ineffectual.

However, we believe that just like the adventurers of old – and even of today – Christian leaders must be tough. Christian leadership requires strength, focus, and discipline. Christian leadership often upsets the status quo – and a few people along with it.

I am a strong advocate that all Christians should lead to the best of their ability in every area of society.

The Message Of Freedom In Christ

As a leader, I have learned that leaders must be tough. I have also learned that as a leader I need Jesus.

I've been involved with Freedom In Christ since the early 1990s. Integrating the Freedom In Christ teachings – including *The Freedom In Christ Discipleship Course* – in my life and ministry has been a key factor not only for being able to survive such intense conflict for such a long period of time but also for being able to thrive in the midst of more "ordinary" difficulties. These materials have become foundational to my leadership.

We hope that you have already been through *The Freedom In Christ Discipleship Course*, including *The Steps to Freedom In Christ*. If so, you'll know that the course has three key messages. They apply just as much to your leadership as to your growth in your Christian life.

The first message is "Know the **truth** of who you are in Christ".

As Christians, God has given us a new identity and made us new creations. Knowing who I was in Christ allowed me to avoid so much wounding that many leaders experience. It also helped me to heal more quickly when I was deeply wounded. It gave me confidence to lead as the person God had made me to be.

The second message is "Be aware of the reality of the spiritual world and resolve spiritual issues with **truth**".

As we lead, we need to be aware of the reality of the spiritual world and the enemy who wants to prevent our people living in the abundant life Jesus supplies. Realizing that I was in a spiritual battle helped me recognize that people in my church were not my enemy. Satan was my enemy. I knew that I could not succeed by attacking people, but only by knowing and believing truth. In the end, truth won out.

The third key message is "Be transformed through the renewing of your mind with **truth**".

In my situation, every day I had to renew my mind with the truth as found in the Bible. I was tempted to believe so many lies about my situation, and the

Bible exposed these lies to the truth. Praying the Psalms helped me express myself to God. Reading the Bible reminded me that God is good, no matter what my circumstances.

As Christians, we have a great leadership advantage. Jesus Christ, the greatest leader who ever lived, lives in us by the power of the Holy Spirit. Jesus has destroyed the power of sin, death and hell in the cross and the empty tomb.

Yet sadly, as Christians we often fail to apply these realities to our leadership. We need a greater vision for our leadership as Christians, one that allows us to lead as the people God has created us to be.

Real Christian Leadership

WANTED
REAL
CHRISTIAN
LEADERS

The purpose of this session is to present the course definition of Christian leadership. We will focus on a number of issues involved with our definition including things like styles of leadership, outcomes of leadership and whether leaders are born or made.

DISCUSSION AIMS

Pause For Thought 1 (page 23)

Many people think that they cannot be leaders because they are not "born" leaders. One goal of the session is to help people understand that they are leaders whether or not they are natural leaders.

Pause For Thought 2 (page 28)

In this Pause For Thought, we want people to begin thinking about what makes Christian leadership uniquely "Christian". We also hope that during the discussion many people will have come to realize that they really are leaders.

WORSHIP

- Choose a song focusing on delighting in the Lord or His goodness.
- Read Psalm 37:1–4.
- Express your trust in the Lord.
- Praise God by expressing His goodness and delightfulness.

Notes for participants are on pages 19–30.

The Nature Of Real Christian Leadership

Freed To Lead is specifically about Christian leadership and in this session we are going to try to start to understand what the nature of true Christian leadership is and what makes it distinctively different from other forms of leadership.

A good place to start would be to consider some of the metaphors the Bible uses.

In Luke 22:24–27 the disciples get into an argument about which of them is the greatest. It's really an argument about the nature of true leadership and Jesus' response is very illuminating.

Christian leaders are called to be **servants** of those they lead. This would be completely anathema to the likes of Stalin or many powerful leaders.

Jesus Himself came into the world to serve and anyone who wants to be great in His kingdom will be the servant of all.

In recent years, there's been a recognition in business that really great leaders, the ones who have the greatest effect, are those who genuinely put others before themselves, who put the good of their company before their own interests.

Jesus said to them again, "Peace be with you. As the Father has sent me, even so I am sending you." (John 20:21)

Jesus knew He had been sent by the Father for a particular purpose. And as the Father sent Him, He sends us into the world. We need to know that we are **sent ones**.

Many of you who are in a leadership position right now will know full well that God has called you there. He will have made it abundantly clear. What if you didn't get that clear sense but are in a leadership position? I think you can nevertheless assume that God has called you to be a leader and has specifically sent you to the place where you are leading, whether that's a business, hospital, school, church, or whatever. You can also assume that He has prepared some works in advance for you to do. Exciting!

Some of you don't yet have a leadership position but sense a possible call. If that's what God has in mind for you, He will bring it about in His time. Some of you think, "I could never be a leader." Why ever not? Remember that it's not about external qualifications. He calls and sends **the most unlikely people** – often the ones without the obvious qualifications who feel totally inadequate. Look at how God called David to be king of Israel even though on paper he was the most unlikely candidate.

Knowing that you are specifically called, specifically sent by God, is vital, especially when things get tough.

In the New Testament, the main Greek word that describes leaders is usually translated as "steward" or sometimes "manager". A Christian leader is a **steward**: the place of leadership we have been sent into – our leadership ministry if you like – is not ours but His.

God doesn't need us to do His work. But in His humility He delegates to us the responsibility of managing His resources in order to bear fruit and to advance His kingdom.

A mark of a real Christian leader is that we won't cling to our leadership position but will be ready to lay it down when the time comes. He is the potter – we are the clay.

Christian leaders are also **shepherds**, caring for the people who follow them.

Jesus said, "He who is a hired hand and not a shepherd, who does not own the sheep, sees the wolf coming and leaves the sheep and flees, and the wolf snatches them and scatters them" (John 10:12).

Shepherds look out for the well-being of the sheep, making sure they are fed and protected. A hired hand is in it just for the money and will abandon the sheep when danger comes. But for a true shepherd, it's much more than a paid job. They really care.

> *So you are no longer a slave, but a son, and if a son, then an heir through God.*
>
> *(Galatians 4:7)*

In a large estate in New Testament times such as the one in the story of the prodigal son, both sons and slaves worked. What was the difference between them? A slave works because he has to whereas a **son** works because he chooses to. And a son has all the father's resources freely available to him. You have become a son of God (and that applies to women too!). You can exercise your leadership confident of your heavenly Father's support and encouragement. Those who know they are true sons of God make the very best leaders.

Leaders Are Followers Too

We may be leaders but we won't lead effectively unless we're also good followers.

Jesus said, "Follow me, and I will make you fishers of men" (Matthew 4:19). There's an interesting dynamic there: He called people to follow Him and the result would be that people would listen to **them**, would follow **them**.

The bottom line is that just being a Christian and having a leadership position doesn't make you a real Christian leader. A real Christian leader is someone who gets up every day and makes a decision to follow Jesus. Their relationship with God is so fundamental that it influences everything in their leadership.

They choose to believe that the Bible is the very Word of God – what it says becomes the bottom line in their leadership.

They make a daily choice to be led by the Spirit of God and therefore keep growing in the fruit of the Spirit.

The result is that, slowly but surely, they are becoming more and more like Jesus in character.

Those of you who know Freedom In Christ well may have spotted in there our definition of discipleship: "a disciple is someone who is becoming more and more like Jesus in character." And it is the development of godly character that will lead us more and more to act like Jesus acted. Christian leadership is an issue of discipleship. If we are not following Jesus well, we will not lead others well.

Definition Of Christian Leadership

Let's now try to get to the heart of what Christian leadership actually is. Let me give you our definition:

Christian leadership is the interactive relational process of influencing people and people-systems towards beneficial outcomes through your identity, character, and calling in Christ, using your God-given strengths and spiritual gifts as well as your talents, skills, and knowledge.

That's quite a mouthful but every element is important. We're going to look at each portion of this definition.

Leadership Is A Process

First, leadership is a process. A process is something that is always ongoing, something that is never fully completed. When you are a leader, you can never say "Well, that's it; the job is done!"

Leadership Is Relational

It is always people centred. Although there are many things we do as leaders, we always do them in the context of relationships. Maybe you have joked that your job would be great if it wasn't for the people! Actually, if you have no relationships, then you have no leadership.

Leadership Is Interactive

And this relational process is interactive. What we mean by that is that, in the process of leading, you should expect to be changed just as much or possibly more than the people you lead. If you're not willing to be changed then you probably shouldn't be a leader.

John Maxwell has one of the shortest definitions of leadership – "Leadership is influence" – and he is surely right. But who are you influencing? Our definition says that it's about influencing both people and people-systems. It's easy to assume that if we are able to lead individuals well by influencing them, then we will be successful in our leadership. But there is more to it than that.

Our definition says that the influence is not just on people but also on what we are going to call "people-systems", the groups and organizations of which people are part.

The Outcomes Of Leadership

Christian leaders are leading "towards beneficial outcomes". Not everyone is.

Real Christian leadership ensures that the outcomes of leadership are beneficial to others. Another word for outcomes might be "fruit". Christian leaders want to lead towards good fruit, ideally fruit that will last for eternity.

So, how can we assess whether an outcome is beneficial or not? Here are some questions we can ask:

Does it benefit people economically? All organizations understand financial outcomes. They are the easiest to measure and you do need cash if the organization is to continue. However, most organizations also understand that just making money isn't enough – it's not just about profit. We also need to exercise good stewardship over all our resources. A small church without a minister may generate a lot of money by selling the house it owns, but future generations may never again be able to afford to call a minister and the church may eventually die. Was that really beneficial?

Does it benefit people socially? Does the outcome help create healthy relationships? Does it help build a healthy society? A business may develop a culture in which its employees work so many hours that marriages break down and families fall apart. Even if that business made lots of money, clearly its outcomes are not beneficial.

Does it benefit people environmentally? Of course, this applies to the physical environment in which we live. But this question also applies to the spiritual environment. Things like prayer, worship, repentance and a commitment to unity across churches can change the spiritual environment.

Does it benefit people personally? Christian leaders empower people to take responsibility, to grow, to develop in terms of their character.

Does it benefit people spiritually? Is it in line with God's Kingdom purposes?

Based On Who You Are

The vast majority of books on leadership focus on what good leaders **do**. Christian leadership, however, focuses first on who good leaders **are**. This issue is critical and we'll come back to it in the next session. For now, let me just say this: Leadership involves who you are. Christian leadership involves who you are in Christ.

People will follow who you are and how you are before they will follow what you do or say.

Actually it would perhaps be more precise to say they follow who they **think** you are. If people perceive you to be a leader they will follow you. You can see this in how some people follow celebrities – quite literally when it comes to social media. When last I checked, the person with the most followers on a popular social media platform was a singer I had never heard of. Next came a singer I had heard of. Does being a popular singer say anything about the soundness of your opinions? Probably not. But people follow celebrities because of who they appear to be, even though that might be an identity crafted by a clever PR machine.

Jesus was the most compelling leader who ever lived. Why? Because of who He was. His followers can become compelling leaders too – because of who He has made them to be.

Born Or Made?

The definition continues: "Using your God-given strengths and spiritual gifts as well as your talents, skills, and knowledge."

You are a unique person with a unique set of gifts and strengths. You also have weaknesses. If you want to achieve excellence in leadership, which should you focus on, your strengths or your weaknesses?

You can spend so much time trying to compensate for your weaknesses that you never get round to using your strengths. Yet your strengths are what enable you to become an effective leader. Focusing on what you don't do well is a recipe for mediocrity.

Great leaders discover what they do well and then do it to the best of their ability. Focus on your strengths and see if you can delegate the other things to people who have strengths in those areas.

Now, let's consider a big question: are some people given the gift of being able to lead and others not? Can anyone be a leader, or is it reserved for a select few people?

In other words, are leaders born? Or are they made?

Surely it's both! Some people just have a propensity to lead. They can't help but lead because it is their natural disposition. We call these people "natural leaders".

That doesn't, however, necessarily make them the best leaders.

Other people have to lead because to their great surprise they find themselves called to a leadership role. They may not be natural leaders but there's no reason whatsoever why they shouldn't be great leaders. Whether you're a natural leader or not, you can learn how to improve your leadership and become a great leader.

Does anyone need to come out of the shadows at this point? Do you need to recognize, perhaps for the first time, that God has called you to your leadership position? And that He is well able to make you the leader He wants you to be?

This brings us to our leadership dilemma – our challenge without an easy solution.

We tend to think that becoming a better leader is all about improving our leadership style or trying to look like what we think a "natural" leader looks like. However, those are not the things that will make us great leaders.

There has been a tendency in the last couple of decades for the Church to adopt secular leadership principles and I'm not knocking that. There are some really helpful things there. But our heart is to see it going the other way. We want the world to see that real Christian leadership is the most effective leadership there is. So that headhunters actively seek out Christians for key leadership roles.

Because real Christian leadership is the type of leadership that every organization everywhere needs.

Our vision is to see genuinely Christian leadership not just in homes and churches but in business, in politics, in the health service, and in education. Everywhere!

Being And Doing

The purpose of this session is to present the being and doing dynamic that is at the core of identity-based leadership.

Pause For Thought 1 (page 34)

In this Pause For Thought, we want people to begin thinking about other leaders they have enjoyed following. The goal is that they might use what they have enjoyed in other leaders to help shape their own leadership.

Pause For Thought 2 (page 44)

The goal of this Pause For Thought is to determine whether or not people understand the basic message of the session – that our doing as leaders flows from our being as leaders. It is also good for people to see how the influence of the world and the flesh especially have held them back in their understanding and practice of leadership.

- Choose a song that focuses on trusting the Lord or on His righteousness and justice.
- Read Psalm 37:5–8.
- Wait silently before the Lord for several minutes.
- Thank God that He will act on your behalf and that he will make your righteousness and justice shine.

Notes for participants are on pages 31–44.

Being And Doing

We've already noted that people will follow who you are and how you are before they will follow what you do or say. In this session we're going to look a little more at the critical relationship between who we are – our "being" – and what we do – our "doing".

We know that salvation is God's gift of grace and we say something like this to people, "Come to Jesus just as you are and lay your burdens at the foot of the cross. You don't have to do anything. Just come." They respond.

"Now," we say, "You need to learn to be a disciple. Read your Bible every day, come to the mid-week meeting, come to church on Sunday." All good things to do but it can become a kind of subtle Christian behaviourism – try this, try not to do that.

We've learned that the key to helping someone become a fruitful disciple is not to teach them what to **do** but to teach them who they **are**, what happened to them the moment they came to Christ. So that it is not a "trying harder" mentality – it's about realizing what has already happened and working from that point.

Think of the last leadership book you read, Christian or not. Was it about being or doing? I strongly suspect it was about doing. "If you want to be a better leader, do this, try this... Here's a technique you can try or a system you can implement."

We are wired to "do" and we naturally assume that our behaviour is the primary issue. Yet what we have discovered in both discipleship and leadership is that the primary issue is not doing, it's **being**.

It's primarily about what is inside, what Jesus calls your "heart" and what we are calling your being. The point is this: **your doing will always flow from your being**. If your being is good, your doing will be good. If your being is bad, your doing will ultimately be bad.

Yes, people followed the Pharisees, but what were the outcomes of their leadership? Jesus said, "They are blind guides. And if the blind lead the blind, both will fall into a pit" (Matthew 15:14). All negative. Their doing might have looked fantastic and they may have used all the latest techniques but their being was wrong.

Being And Doing In Leadership

So let's consider what we mean by "being" in a leader, and to start with we're talking about any leader, Christian or not. What makes up their "being"?

They have a unique mind, will and emotions; and a unique temperament: introvert, extrovert, thinker, feeler, or whatever. They have a unique background: influenced by their culture, gender, upbringing, and experiences. And they have a unique mixture of natural abilities, strengths and weaknesses, and hopes and dreams. Those things make up their "being".

And out of their being will come what they do. Things like making choices, taking action, building relationships. These things are their "doing".

This being/doing dynamic is something that operates in every leader. If you want to improve your leadership but just focus on trying to modify your behaviour without looking at what is inside, ultimately you won't get very far. People will see through it because there's only so long you can modify your behaviour before reverting back to your true character.

So, leadership involves both who you are and what you do. Being is about your identity, character, and calling. Doing refers to your actions and choices. Your doing flows from your being – always. If your being is not right, your doing will not lead in a healthy way.

The Advantage Of Being A Christian Leader

So if you want to be the leader God is calling you to be, first and foremost you have to focus on getting your being right.

This is where Christian leaders have a massive advantage. What we've just talked about applies to any leader. But if you are a Christian, there's a more fundamental part to your being that not-yet-Christians just don't have.

The moment you came to Christ, you became a brand new creation. You became spiritually alive. Your spirit was connected to God's spirit. And you have been made holy deep down inside. Paul tells us that Jesus **became** sin for us so that we could actually **become** the righteousness of God (2 Corinthians 5:21).

This means that at the most fundamental level your being is inherently right. As good as it possibly could be. Holy. Righteous. And all without your doing a single thing.

You are forgiven, accepted, and pleasing to God. You now have the Holy Spirit within you so that you can be and do everything that God has called you to be and do. "This is my son with whom I am well pleased!" was what God said to Jesus. When? Right at the start of His ministry – before He had done a single thing! It's the same for you. God takes pleasure in you primarily for who you now **are** not for what you **do**. He looks at your being and loves it!

Only Christian leaders have the opportunity to start at the place where their being is absolutely right. And that should influence your "doing" very positively. How could it not?

You are not a second class leader. You are not somehow leading under false pretences. You are a child of God and He has called you to a significant work in His Kingdom that you can do because of who you are in Christ.

Enemies Of Real Christian Leadership

Just being a Christian with a holy being doesn't automatically make you an authentic Christian leader. It just gives you the best possible start. There's more to your being than the fact that you have become a new creation – your character needs to be constantly developing and maturing so that you become more and more like Jesus. But that is now completely possible. The outcome depends very much on you and the choices you make.

Just as with Christian discipleship, the things that can hold us back are our old enemies, the world, the flesh, and the devil.

The World Can Hold Us Back

Most of the time when you see dysfunctional leadership in the Church it is because we have leaders who are Christians but who don't really know who they are in Christ.

The world wants us to rely on things such as status and position for our sense of identity and encourages us to look to our leadership position to get our sense of worth rather than to who we now are in Christ.

To the degree that you base your identity in your leadership position, your leadership will be distorted, dysfunctional, or less effective.

When difficulties come, leaders who have not resolved this issue, often resort to saying in effect, "Follow me because I'm the leader." Jesus was the Son of God Himself but he never felt the need to tell people that. They wanted to follow Him because His being was right not because of His position. Remember, people will follow who you are and how you are before they will follow what you do or say.

God is not measuring you by your job level, the size of the team you lead, the outward trappings of success or any other external factor. He has one concern: your character, the extent to which you are becoming more and more like Jesus.

The Devil Can Hold Us Back

It is knowing – really knowing – the truth about our being that will set us free to lead effectively. But the Father of Lies wants to keep us from knowing the truth. Those of us brought up in the West are predisposed to overlook the reality of the spiritual world. Although we acknowledge it intellectually and theologically, when it comes to living our lives and leading our team, we can act as though we are living in a world that is purely physical. Big mistake!

Paul is clear that if you let the sun go down on your anger – if you sin – you give the devil a foothold, a place of influence, in your life (Ephesians 4:26). And that makes it much more difficult to know the truth. The battleground is our mind, our thinking. The battle is all about truth and lies.

The way to resolve these footholds is through repentance, which in practice means submitting to God and resisting the devil (James 4:7).

The Flesh Can Hold Us Back

Even though we are now holy deep down inside, we can lead like someone whose being has not been made holy. Galatians 5:16 says, "Live by the Spirit, and you will not gratify the desires of the flesh." But it's a daily choice. We are either walking according to the promptings of the Spirit or the urges of the flesh.

We can be deceived into believing lies about our leadership. For example, a common lie we believe is thinking that the outcome depends on us so we end up leading in our own strength.

Maturing as a Christian and becoming an effective Christian leader both have a lot to do with uncovering faulty ways of thinking that have developed over the years as we have fallen for the lies of the world, the flesh, and the devil.

All of us have been "programmed" in different ways but can now choose to change that programming. It takes some effort over a period of time but Paul says in Romans 12:2 that it is in renewing our minds that we will be transformed. As you go through this course, our prayer is that your eyes will be opened to areas where your belief system is not in line with truth. As you become aware of them, we'd encourage you to write them down.

If you've been through The Freedom In Christ Discipleship Course, you will know that we have a method called "Stronghold-Busting" to enable you to take a structured approach to getting rid of lies and believing the truth.

You work out what the faulty belief is: for example, that the outcome depends on my own efforts alone. Then you turn to the Bible and find what is really true, verses such as "I can do nothing on my own" and you write a declaration. I renounce the lie that the outcome depends on my own efforts. I announce the truth that I can do nothing on my own but I can do all things through Him who gives me strength. Then you make your declaration for forty days or so, which is the time it takes to change a habitual way of thinking. It's like swinging a demolition ball against a wall time and time again. For ages nothing seems to change but eventually the cracks appear and the wall comes down. You really are transformed by the renewal of your mind and this is an effective way to do that.

Character Is The Key

As you learn to focus on living out of your being which has been made righteous, you will grow in godly character. The evidence for this will be more and more of the fruit of the Spirit in your life – love, joy, peace, patience, kindness, goodness, faithfulness, gentleness, and self-control (Galatians 5:22–23).

Maturity shows when you are increasingly willing to take responsibility for your own mind, will, and emotions, and make good choices.

You will increasingly love others and want to serve them in humility rather than seeing leadership as a way to get your needs met or to build your ego.

You will increasingly see a consistency between the internal and external – what you see is what you get. You will have no need to try to hide what is inside. Others will experience this as integrity.

Brokenness And Fruitfulness

For that reason, part of God's preparation for real Christian leaders is brokenness. God so wants us to know the truth that we can do nothing on our own and to help us stay in that place of dependence that, in his love for us, He sometimes unleashes events in our lives that overwhelm us, that take us out of our depth and into realms where we find ourselves beyond our ability to cope.

God did it with Paul. He sent him something that troubled him – maybe a health issue, we don't know. Paul just called it a thorn in the flesh. He prayed three times that God would take it away but God refused and simply said, "My grace is sufficient for you, for my power is made perfect in weakness," to which Paul responded, "Therefore I will boast all the more gladly of my weaknesses, so that the power of Christ may rest upon me." (2 Corinthians 12:9)

He uses all sorts of things: loss of reputation, personal conflict, or financial difficulties perhaps. Whatever it is, it will be tailor-made to get down to the issues that need resolving in our being and to get us back to that place of knowing that we are truly dependent on Him, that we can do nothing on our own.

Leadership Also Involves Doing

Let me emphasize again that we are not saying that leadership is about being rather than doing. It is about both. You can be a good person but a very poor leader. You can know your identity in Christ but fail to lead others.

All leadership – effective and ineffective, godly and ungodly – involves both who you are and what you do. Our point is simply this: your doing flows from your being. Always. If your being is not right, your doing will not lead in a healthy way.

So you will also need to focus on what you do and there are always lots of things for leaders to do: deciding, discerning, directing, developing, delegating, disciplining... did you notice that they all begin with D? If you find yourself doing anything that does not begin with D, stop immediately!

Neither are we saying that various techniques will not work. Doing certain things will always lead others. The question is not whether you are leading people but where you are leading them to, whether or not the outcomes are beneficial.

Leadership Styles And Theories

There are any number of different leadership styles and theories out there. Most of them focus on doing rather than being but that doesn't mean that they are of no value. By all means use them.

The crucial thing to remember, however, is that the particular theory or style of leadership leaders may choose is not as important as the leader themselves. If your being is not right, none of these things will help you lead as God desires or intends.

Let's finish with a couple of key verses regarding our doing that highlight a leadership dilemma:

Jesus, even though He was the Son of God, said: "I can do nothing on my own" (John 5:30). Some of us have to work against the tendency to forge ahead and do things in our strength. We have to recognize that we can do nothing of any lasting value on our own.

Paul said: "I can do all things through him who strengthens me" (Philippians 4:13).

Others of us have to work against the tendency not to do anything and hang back too much – maybe because we still feel that we are not really "a leader" or out of cowardice, laziness or an unwillingness to take responsibility.

We can have a tendency either to forge ahead and do things in our strength, or to hang back too much and not do what we should. The biblical principle is: I can do "all things" but only "through him who strengthens me".

If you know Jesus, you have been given the best possible start as a leader because you have a new perfect being! As your character grows to become more and more like Him, it will work its way out into your doing.

The bottom line is this: there is nothing whatsoever to stop you becoming the leader Jesus wants you to be and playing your part in seeing society transformed.

Leading In Your Context

The purpose of this session is to present one of the contexts of leadership known as "people-systems". We will show that leaders must focus on people-systems as well as individuals in order to lead effectively.

DISCUSSION AIMS

Pause For Thought 1 (page 48)

In this Pause For Thought, we want people to begin seeing how factors external to themselves – such as the behaviour of other people and the context they are leading in – affect how easy or difficult it is to lead.

Pause For Thought 2 (page 52)

The goal of this Pause For Thought is to determine how well people understand the concept of a people-system. We want people to see how people-systems affect leadership. We also want people to see how their leadership might influence whole groups of people instead of just individuals.

WORSHIP

- Choose a song that focuses on God's sovereignty.
- Read Psalm 37:9–13.
- Thank God that wickedness and wrongdoing shall not prevail.
- Thank God that His people will inherit the land – that is, become people of influence throughout your city, region, or nation.

Notes for participants are on pages 45–54.

People-Systems

One of the most overlooked factors affecting our leadership is the context of our leadership. We don't lead in isolation. Leadership always operates in a context. The context will determine our leadership effectiveness as much as our actions do. One of our great delusions is that we can lead effectively no matter where we are.

One important context of leadership is what we call a "people-system". Essentially, any system is a just set of things working together as a complex whole.

So a people-system is any set or group of people with a connectedness from which its own identity and forms emerge. As people associate together in groups, they naturally begin to develop a common sense of identity and certain ways of doing things. This group quickly begins to take on a life of its own, becoming a complex unit with an existence distinct from its individual members. This group has become a people-system.

The most basic people-system is the human family. However, wherever people connect together in groups they form a people-system. This is a natural tendency among all human beings. God created us this way.

These groups determine our leadership effectiveness much more than we realise. Effective leaders are always leaders of people-systems.

In the New Testament, the concept of "household" is an example of a people-system. "Household" can refer to a family, a business, or even the church itself.

In the Old Testament, God often referred to whole nations as one large individual people-system by using a singular name, such as Ephraim, Edom, or Egypt. The prophet Amos spends three chapters calling out the sins of nations as if they were the sins of individuals.

Paul himself even compares the people-system called the church to another well-known system: the human body.

God designed us as social beings, so we naturally group ourselves together. These groups quickly become living entities themselves. We spontaneously organise ourselves with a clear identity and defined ways of relating. After this, we begin to receive a sense of personal satisfaction and meaning from our association with these groups. We learn and grow from our connections with these groups. We tend to conform our behaviour to what is acceptable to the group.

When they're healthy, people-systems will influence us toward behaviour that is good and virtuous. This explains why the church is so important to effective discipleship. These people-systems then become the foundation for a healthy society.

Leaders In People-Systems

In the Bible, leaders of people-systems were called "stewards". Stewards were leaders with authority, not just "managers" as is often translated. Stewards had a responsibility to lead well and promote good outcomes for their masters.

In healthy people-systems, leadership will rotate among various people depending on the needs of the group at any given moment. However, leaders will always emerge based on how people are behaving within the people-system or based on how people perceive others within the people-system.

This means that if we are behaving like a leader and people are following us then we are leaders – no matter whether we have a title or position. This also means that if people see us as the leader then they will expect us to lead. This dynamic works negatively as well: if people don't see us as the leader or don't follow us, then no matter what title or position we may have, and no matter what we think we are, we're not the leader.

People-Systems As "Persons"
Brain

In people-systems, leaders function much like brains function in the human body. Through our being, we regulate the healthy functioning of the people-system, much as the brain regulates the heart beating or the breathing of the body. Through our doing, we help the people-system make good choices and take wise actions, much as the brain determines what we say and do. The key point is this: **Our being as leaders influences our people-systems more deeply and profoundly than we realize. It is our primary leadership influence in our people-system.**

Paul's comparison of the church with a human body gives us great insights not only into the church but also into all people-systems.

From this we would suggest that a people-system might be roughly compared to an individual person, having a spirit, a soul, and a body. The soul includes the mind, emotions, and will. As leaders, we need to understand how we influence all these aspects of the people-system both through our being and through our doing.

Spirit

People-systems have what we might call a "spirit". The spirit of a people-system is an invisible dynamic that emanates from the people-system and influences people within and around it, much like a gravitational field emanates from a planet.

So the spirit of a people-system describes that invisible reality which influences and affects people within its range socially and spiritually. The spirit of a system gives it a sense of life and vitality.

The spirit of a people-system operates in accordance with spiritual principles. Sin and legalism bring death to the spirit. Repentance and forgiveness bring life to the spirit. If we sow to the flesh in a people-system we will reap corruption. If we sow to the Spirit we will reap life.

As a spiritual reality, the spirit of a system may be influenced by the Holy Spirit, angels, or demons. As a spiritual reality, the spirit of a people-system may also be influenced by spiritual activities such as prayer, worship, Bible reading, and thanksgiving.

Paul is very aware of this spiritual reality. In Colossians 2, Paul cautions the church about the elemental spirits of the world that may influence them corporately.

In Ephesians 6, Paul tells us that we are wrestling against principalities and powers – spiritual forces that influence people-systems. In Ephesians 4, Paul tells the church to remember they are all members of one body and so they should not give the devil a foothold.

Because of the spiritual dynamic of people-systems, **the past influences the present in the people-system**. What has happened in the past influences what happens today. The good legacy of the past will influence the people-system towards beneficial outcomes. The sin of the past will influence the people-system in ways contrary to God's will.

This is why it's important for a people-system to celebrate the good of its past while repenting of the sins of the past. Repentance in this context simply means that we acknowledge what happened was sinful and then we make a conscious choice not to continue the sins of the past into the present.

As leaders, we influence the spirit of the people-system through our being and doing. Our connection with our people-system means that our spiritual health and integrity as leaders will naturally promote spiritual health and integrity in the system. Our relationship with God will naturally help the people-system connect with God. This is true in the marketplace as well as in the church.

When we as leaders engage in activities such as prayer, worship, repentance, forgiveness, and thanksgiving on our own and with others, we influence the spirit of the people-system – even when we do these things in the workplace. As we resolve the sin issues of the past and embrace the positive spiritual heritage of the past publicly, we shape the spirit of the people-system.

Soul

The soul of a people-system has three parts: emotions, mind, and will.

Emotions, or what we might call "emotional processes", are constantly active in people-systems. Emotional processes are the complex interplay of our impressions, feelings, and inclinations, and those of everyone around us, which influences our thoughts, emotions, and choices. Like our human emotions, emotional processes happen automatically.

This dynamic happens continuously in any people-system. Whether the emotional processes are positive or negative will determine how well people hear us and respond to us. They will determine how people relate to one another.

As leaders, our being and doing influence the emotional processes of our people-system. If we are emotionally healthy and have good emotional awareness, our health will help to create and regulate healthy emotional processes. If we are positive and set a hopeful tone, then we will help build healthy emotional reactions in our people-system. How we react emotionally to things going on will help determine how other people react.

As leaders, we can choose to remain calm and connected with people even when they are not calm. We can choose joy. We can express appropriate humour. We can be optimistic. All these things will influence the emotions of our people-system.

Groups seem to develop a **mind** of their own. This happens in families, churches, businesses, and even nations. This is a natural phenomenon.

It is also biblical. In places like Philippians 2:5, 1 Peter 3:8, and Romans 12:1–2, the Bible uses the singular word "mind" in a collective sense. So when we are told that we have the "mind of Christ", Paul is telling us that together as one people-system we have the mind of Christ.

In a sense, our battle is a battle for the mind of our people-system. Just like people, people-systems can develop mental strongholds that influence them contrary to the will of God. Just like people, we need to renew our people-system mind with truth. This is why activities such as preaching and studying the Bible are so essential for churches.

As leaders, our being influences the mind of our people-system. If we are mature and reflect the fruit of the Spirit in our character, then our people-system will begin to embrace that same maturity.

What we focus on personally as leaders will determine the focus of our people-system. If we as leaders value the Bible and ensure that the Bible conditions how we think, then the people we lead will naturally begin to do the same, even in the marketplace.

Our doing as leaders will direct the focus of the people we lead. The sermons we preach – or, in the case of the marketplace, the messages we send – the perspectives we have and how we engage in thinking and reasoning publicly will all influence the mind of our system.

This is why having a vision is so important for a leader. If you have a vision and you keep yourself focused on that vision then your vision will naturally influence the vision of your people-system. Your whole system will naturally move toward the vision.

People-systems also have a **will**. They make corporate choices and decisions. Voting is one common way that people-systems express their will, but there are many others. The choices and decisions of the people-system will reflect the true values of that people-system.

How people-systems exercise their collective will tells us a lot about the people-system. For example, all churches will tell us that outreach and prayer are very important, perhaps the most important activities of churches. But many churches do very little outreach or prayer. They may tell us what they think they value but how they exercise their will shows what they really value.

The spirit, emotions or mind of the system lead the will of the system. They determine how a system chooses and acts. So if we try to change the will of the system before we change the spirit, emotions or mind of the system, then we will almost always fail.

As leaders, we influence the will of our people-system, too. In our being, we must remain well connected to the people-system. We must also be determined to persevere when people in the system don't do what we think they should right away.

In our doing, we need to model healthy choices and healthy relationships. If we want people to make difficult choices, then we must first make those difficult choices for ourselves. If we want our people-system to anchor its choices in the Bible, then we must anchor our choices in the Bible and let people see how we do this.

The spirit, emotions, mind and will of the people-system are constantly interacting with one another. They influence each other continuously just like they do in us as individuals.

Body

Systems also have what we might call a "body", or "flesh and bones". The flesh and bones of a system includes things like the structures created by the system (such as buildings), the policies and procedures they develop (such as constitutions), the ways the people-system portrays itself to the world (such as websites), and how the members of the people-system interface with one another (such as small groups and work teams).

The flesh and bones of a people-system are an expression of the interplay of the spirit, soul, and leadership of the people-system. Once the flesh and bones of a people-system matures and takes shape, it will itself influence the spirit, soul, and leadership of the system.

One of the greatest mistakes we leaders make is assuming that we can lead by changing the flesh and bones of a people-system. We assume if we have the right structure in place then people will naturally conform to it. This never happens. The history of churches, businesses, and nations are filled with stories of leaders who failed because they tried to lead by first changing the flesh and bones of their people-system.

We will help shape the flesh and bones of our people-systems by promoting health and positive change in the spirit and soul of the system first. This will create a desire in the system to change the flesh and bones of the system. Our attitude must be one of understanding and respect towards the flesh and bones of the system as a legacy of the past even as we desire to change the flesh and bones of the system for the future.

The spirit, soul, and body of a people-system constantly influence the people within that system. They enable people-systems to become agents of transformation in people's lives – for better or for worse. Our major influence as leaders will be to influence the spirit and soul of our people-systems through our being, not just our doing. That's why healthy leadership is essential for a healthy people-system.

This leads us to our leadership dilemma:

Becoming a healthy leader is one of our greatest responsibilities. Yet being a healthy leader alone does not determine our fruitfulness as a leader. A healthy people-system will often help make an unhealthy leader effective; an unhealthy people-system will often render a healthy leader ineffective. This means that our people-system will determine our leadership effectiveness far more than we realize.

Our next session will consider how to address this.

Building Healthy People-Systems

The purpose of this session is to help people identify the characteristics of a healthy people-system as opposed to a sick people-system. The session will also introduce one of the most common sicknesses that affects people-systems: anxiety.

DISCUSSION AIMS

Pause For Thought 1 (page 58)

We have two goals in this Pause For Thought. First, we want people to see the qualities that will undermine their leadership effectiveness. Second, we want people to begin thinking about how they can determine health in any group of people.

Pause For Thought 2 (page 65)

The goal of this Pause For Thought is to help people begin to diagnose sickness and dysfunction in people-systems. Many times, people do not recognize that a people-system is sick so they do not take steps to bring healing.

WORSHIP

- Choose a song that focuses on how God provides for His people.
- Read Psalm 37:14–16.
- Thank God for how He cares for the poor and needy and how He provides for His people.

Notes for participants are on pages 55–67.

Healthy People-Systems

Our leadership must have three hallmarks for us to promote health in our people-systems. First, as we have discussed already, our being must be healthy and grounded in our relationship with Jesus Christ.

Second, we need genuine humility. We need a sober, truth-filled view of ourselves. We also need to know the greatness of our God.

Third, we need a holy determination to see our people-systems become healthy. We cannot quit easily if we want to bring health to a people-system. Health requires time and effort, especially if we're beginning from a place of unhealthiness.

On top of this, it also helps to know how to recognize healthy people-systems and what distinguishes them from unhealthy people-systems.

Healthy people-systems have three characteristics, no matter whether they are churches, businesses, or governments. The first characteristic is **mutual submission**, as expressed in Ephesians 5:21. It's the spirit of co-operation with one another so that together we achieve beneficial outcomes.

The second characteristic is **unity**, such as that found in Psalm 133 and Ephesians 4:3. Unity is a sense of cohesiveness and coherence. People are committed to one another and are committed to staying together and working together. Unity comes from having the same mind and the same values according to 1 Corinthians 1:10.

The third characteristic is **love**, as Paul says in Colossians 3:14. Love is a zealous, self-giving commitment to others for their well-being. It's a sense of altruism, working for God's best for everyone.

These characteristics cross cultures. When people-systems embody these characteristics they are healthy. They will have a positive influence on other people. And they will naturally tend to promote beneficial outcomes.

Unhealthy People-Systems

There are also three characteristics of unhealthy people-systems. The first is **rebelliousness**, when people refuse to co-operate with one another and instead make demands and insist on their own way.

The second is **factionalism**, where people split off from others and form opposing groups. A major indicator of factionalism is secrets, gossip, and rumour-mongering. When you have these, you have factions.

The third characteristic is **selfism**, a radical sense of selfishness in the people-system. Selfishness can be expressed by the whole people-system or by individuals within the people-system.

Building Healthy People-Systems

One of the highest responsibilities we have as leaders is to help create and build healthy people-systems. Although people-systems greatly influence our leadership effectiveness, for good or for ill, we have a tremendous ability from God to influence our people-systems. Healthy people-systems will help build healthy people and help create a healthy society.

Here is a key point: as leaders, the power we have to influence our people-system flows from our being. With our being grounded in Jesus, we will naturally influence our people-system to become healthy and stay healthy.

Our being, more than anything we do, helps to set the mood and tone for our people-system. Our being grounded in Jesus will naturally and favourably regulate the spiritual, emotional, and thinking processes of our people-system.

Our level of influence depends on whether we as leaders are healthy and whether we are genuinely connected and committed to our people-system.

Becoming a leader sometimes feels like getting married to our people-system. Although most of us don't make life-long vows to our people-system, the commitments we make seem similar to marriage vows at times. In most weddings, the husband and wife commit to one another "in sickness and in health". If we're to have a lasting influence in our people-systems as leaders, we also must commit to our systems in sickness and in health.

We have focused mostly on health so far, but we need to remember that, just as a person can get sick, so people-systems can get sick. As leaders, God has given us a huge ability to recognize and resist sickness in our people-system. When our people-systems become ill, our health as leaders will help nurture our people-systems back to health. Our healthy being as leaders will even help our systems resist sickness in the first place.

The Bane Of Leadership – Anxiety

There are many diseases our people-systems might contract, but we want to focus on one of the most pervasive sicknesses for people-systems in the world today. This sickness affects people-systems, people in the systems and leaders alike. It's so pervasive that it's rather like the common cold. And like the common cold there are many things we can do as leaders to resist the sickness and bring health when it strikes.

This sickness is something we call "anxiety".

A book I came across helped me see things from a new perspective. The book is called *A Failure Of Nerve*, by Edwin Friedman. Friedman was writing the book in the late 1990s but he could have been writing it just yesterday. Friedman introduced me to the concept of anxiety and the effect that it had on people and people-systems. What we share about anxiety owes a lot to Friedman's work.

Most people tend to dismiss anxiety as little more than an annoyance. Many people have no idea how pervasive anxiety actually is. Anxiety is endemic in the world today. Anxiety is the unavoidable by-product of the times in which we live. Being overloaded and unfocused produces anxiety. Anxiety plays a major role in many illnesses, both physical and mental. Anxiety is one of the major reasons for the breakdown of many families and churches. And anxiety is partly responsible for the dysfunction that we see in our government and many other organizations of society. It's not just a personal issue; it's a social issue.

So what do we mean by "anxiety"? We have a simple definition: "Anxiety is the painful and disturbing unease or apprehension that stems from inappropriate concern about something uncertain."

Sometimes, anxiety is episodic – it comes up when we face a certain crisis or difficult situation. As soon as the crisis is over, the anxiety goes away. That's fairly normal for everyone. We call this "acute" anxiety.

For many people and people-systems today, anxiety becomes an ongoing part of life. It becomes almost habitual, affecting us continually. We call this "chronic" anxiety. It's this chronic anxiety that has such a destructive influence on people and people-systems.

The Bible has quite a lot to say about anxiety. In 2 Timothy 1:7, Paul tells Timothy that God has not given us a spirit of cowardice. Some versions translate the word as "fear" or "timidity". The word is difficult to translate accurately. The word might be better understood as "a cowardice or failure of nerve that comes from anxiety".

In 1 Peter 5:6–9, Peter points out the connection between anxiety and the demonic. The implication is that anxiety makes Christians susceptible to demonic attack. Clearly, anxiety is a big issue.

In biblical Greek, the word often translated as "anxiety" actually has a range of meanings. The word can be translated "anxiety", or it can be translated as "concern". It has the same range of meaning as the word "care" does in English.

Care or anxiety describes an emotional state that causes us to attach importance to something. When we care about something, we believe it's important. When we're anxious about something, that too indicates it's important to us.

"Care" is a natural emotion like anger which indicates something that needs to be addressed. Whether we translate the word as "care" or "anxiety" depends on the context. Whether we care about something or we're anxious about something, the primary issue is truth. Taking a caring action or resolving anxiety both require a truth-filled response in obedience to God's Word.

Roots Of Anxiety
In order to resolve anxiety, it's helpful to know why people become so anxious in the first place. If we don't have a strong sense of identity and integrity, then we'll be subject to anxiety. If we don't have appropriate confidence in ourselves, then we'll struggle with anxiety.

When we're overloaded and confused, we'll struggle with anxiety. If we don't feel able to process all the information we receive, then we may live with the constant sense that we're missing something important – a feeling of anxiety.

Whenever we face the possibility of loss we'll feel anxious. We call this "loss aversion".

If we place our trust in people and things that aren't God, then we'll suffer from anxiety. The Bible calls this "idolatry".

When we fail to take responsibility for something which we're responsible for, we'll struggle with anxiety. If we don't pay our bills, even if we hide them in a drawer somewhere, then we will suffer from anxiety – no matter how much we struggle to ignore it.

Likewise, if we try to take responsibility for something that is not our responsibility, then we'll struggle with anxiety.

Finally, if we believe lies about ourselves, our situations, our people-systems or God, then we will wrestle with anxiety. As I mentioned, anxiety is primarily an issue of truth.

Features Of Anxiety

Leaders need to understand five important features of anxiety if we're to correctly discern and overcome anxiety.

First, anxiety is infectious. It's a social disease. It naturally spreads from person to person because of the emotional processes we saw in the last session. The more intense the anxiety, the more it will spread. Many people are unaware of this aspect of anxiety.

Second, anxiety hides or disguises itself. It's amazing how much people will deny that they are anxious. Some people will disguise their anxiety as appropriate concern. Because of this, leaders don't recognize how pervasive anxiety might be in their systems. We should expect anxiety to be working in almost every situation we face. But it will be hidden.

Third, anxiety distorts everything. Anxiety distorts our perspectives, communications and perceptions of reality.

Fourth, anxiety weakens the natural defences in both people and people-systems. Anxiety makes people and people-systems susceptible to the influence of outside forces. Anxious people are highly suggestible. For example, much advertising depends on influencing anxious people to buy things they don't need. People will often buy expensive warranties on inexpensive products because they feel anxious that the product might break down.

Finally, and most importantly, anxiety is resistible. Peter tells us to cast all our anxieties on God because he is the one who cares for us. Healthy people in healthy people-systems can resist and resolve anxiety as they renew their minds, demolish strongholds, take appropriate responsibility, and maintain healthy processes.

Anxiety And The Demonic

We need to recognize that anxiety is a spiritual dynamic as well as an emotional dynamic if we are to overcome it. Demons, including principalities and powers, seek to produce, magnify, and manipulate anxiety in people and people-systems in order to control them. As we said, anxiety makes people highly susceptible to outside influences.

Left unresolved, anxiety will give a foothold for the demonic in any person or people-system. We as leaders must often confront these spiritual aspects of anxiety in order to resolve anxiety.

Recognizing Anxiety

We need to learn how to recognize when anxiety is at work.

Let me give you a picture of anxiety at work, using a number of the symptoms: Anxiety wears down our mind, will, and emotions, interfering with our ability to communicate. We begin to feel helpless and defensive. We feel very restless. We try to alleviate these symptoms by seeking quick fixes and engaging in the "too much" syndrome – eating too much, drinking too much, watching too much TV. The more anxiety we have, the worse these effects are.

When we're caught up in chronic anxiety, we can become extremely stubborn, selfish, and very critical. We refuse to take responsibility for problems, but instead we blame everyone else, even if it makes no sense at all. We might even begin engaging in highly destructive behaviours, such as rumours, personal attacks and bullying. Like a volcano, these behaviours will erupt from time to time, spewing over everyone.

When a people-system is struggling with anxiety, people run away from any kind of difficulty and tolerate all sorts of immaturity and poor behaviour.

People will try any fad that comes along, as long as it's easy and helps them feel better. The system loses its sense of mission, and becomes inward focused. People harp on about rights and rules, and exaggerate any issue that might come up. People are always complaining, but their complaints have little substance. They also struggle to work out their issues rationally.

When the people-system's anxiety becomes chronic, people tend to fixate on what or whom they perceive to be the problem, and then they tend to gather in factions with others who think or feel the same way. They fixate on peripheral issues like health and safety. They begin to develop totally unrealistic expectations, but refuse to look at these rationally. They ultimately begin attacking one another personally, especially leaders, using all sorts of ugly language.

If you think through the above symptoms, you might quickly identify quite a number of people-systems caught up in anxiety, perhaps even your own business or church.

Static In Communication

When anxiety is present, it always hinders good communication. It distorts all our communication so that people don't hear or say what they think they hear or say. It causes people to put a pessimistic spin on communication, so even positive words can take on a negative meaning. Anxiety hinders all our attempts to communicate well.

Personal, face-to-face communication is always best, especially when anxiety is present. But we must remain calm as we communicate and make sure people understand what we say.

Obviously, all this anxiety corrodes and weakens leadership. Anxiety inhibits real leadership. To the degree that we have unmanaged or unresolved anxiety, we cannot lead effectively.

If we as leaders have anxiety, then our anxiety will be multiplied in the people-system that we lead. Anxiety in the leader always produces or magnifies anxiety in the people-system. This is true no matter how well we think we can hide our anxiety.

When people-systems are anxious, they always resist leadership. Sometimes, they will do everything they can to remove the leader.

This session leaves us with another leadership dilemma.

As healthy leaders, we might shape and transform our people-system until the people-system becomes healthy also. But only if we survive long enough! Unhealthy systems will often expel healthy leaders before we can complete the task.

True leadership is the only way we have of resolving chronic anxiety, whether in people or people-systems. Yet true leadership often intensifies anxiety before leading people and people-systems out of anxiety. Things can seem to get much worse before they get better.

Anxious people who need to experience true leadership will be the ones who consciously or unconsciously seek to undermine, attack, sabotage, and destroy our leadership.

This means that leadership requires love that hurts – especially us as leaders. We need to become anxiety-resistant leaders fully connected with our people-systems in love.

The purpose of this session is to give leaders clear, specific strategies for resolving personal anxiety in themselves.

OBJECTIVE

DISCUSSION AIMS

Note that the first Pause For Thought includes a 5-minute exercise. You will need to make sure you have a means to time this and also take it into account in your timing plan.

Pause For Thought 1 (page 74)

In this Pause For Thought, we not only want people to practise one of the spiritual disciplines mentioned by Paul in Philippians 4, but we also want people to begin to think how they can intentionally implement these disciplines in their lives. We hope that people will then take steps to do so.

Pause For Thought 2 (page 77)

In this Pause For Thought, we hope that people will be encouraged to take practical steps to resolve their own anxiety. If you have time, you might also like to question participants about their understanding of the concept of "embracing pain" and how they might do that.

WORSHIP

- Choose a song that focuses on God's protection.
- Read Psalm 37:17–20.
- Thank and praise God for how He cares for, protects, and provides for His people during difficult times.

Notes for participants are on pages 67–78.

Anxiety Definition

Proverbs 12:25 says, "Anxiety in a man's heart weighs him down", and so
it does. Last time we defined anxiety as "the painful and disturbing unease
or apprehension that stems from **inappropriate** concern about something
uncertain."

Not all concern is inappropriate. Appropriate concern comes from looking at
a situation realistically – from a truth perspective.

It's when anxiety becomes habitual, an ongoing regular part of life, that it
becomes a problem. The difficulty we face is that anxiety is so widespread
that it appears normal to us and we can be completely unaware just how
much we are affected by it.

A Spiritual Danger

Anxiety gives the enemy a significant opportunity. This is clear from 1 Peter
5:6-8, the passage that Rod referred to in the last session. You may well
have verses 6 and 7 on a bookmark in your bible:

*Humble yourselves, therefore, under the mighty hand of God so that at
the proper time he may exalt you, casting all your anxieties on him,
because he cares for you.*

And you might have the following verse, verse 8, on another bookmark, not
realizing that they are directly linked:

*Be sober-minded; be watchful. Your adversary the devil prowls around
like a roaring lion, seeking someone to devour. (1 Peter 5:6-8)*

Peter quite clearly links not casting your anxieties onto God with the reality that Satan is prowling around looking for someone to devour. Anxiety is a strategy that the enemy is highly likely to try to use against you. Because, if he can tempt you into anxiety, he can affect not just you but your whole people-system.

The bottom line is this: **you can't lead effectively if you are anxious**. Unresolved anxiety in you as a leader will increase the anxiety in your people-system. And if you are struggling with anxiety and find yourself in an anxious people-system, that will increase your anxiety even more. So, before you can address anxiety in the people-system, you must first choose to resolve your own anxiety.

Strategies To Resolve Personal Anxiety

So how do you resolve personal anxiety? The passage gives you two things to do: **humble yourself** and **cast all your anxieties on God**.

1. Humble Yourselves

First we have to humble ourselves under God's mighty hand. Humility is about **letting go of our own agenda** and recognizing that our leadership ministry belongs first and foremost to God. It's about letting go of the false notion that the results are down to our own skills and efforts.

Part of humbling ourselves before God may mean **letting go of wrong goals** we've developed for our lives and for our leadership ministries. What I mean by "goals" in this context is not your current set of business objectives – I'm talking about those things that have become so important to us that we use them to measure our very selves, our sense of success or failure in life or in leadership. All of us are working towards goals but often we don't realize it because they tend to be developed subconsciously.

If you are feeling habitually anxious, it is a strong indication that you may be working towards a goal that feels uncertain to you. The reason any goal feels uncertain is because you can't directly make it happen – its fulfilment depends on people or circumstances that are not under your direct control.

The presence of uncertainty demonstrates that it cannot be a goal that God has given you. Because any goal God gives you **is** under your direct control. Would God ever say in effect, "I have a goal for you. I know you won't be able to fulfil it, but try anyway." Of course not! It's like saying to one of your team, "I want you to double sales by the end of next week. We can't afford any more salespeople and there's no more budget for advertising and promotion but get out there and make it happen!" You wouldn't do that and neither would God.

If a goal you have really is from God, there's nothing uncertain about it. "I can do all things through him who gives me strength" (Philippians 4:13). By definition any goal God has for you can't be blocked by other people or by adverse circumstances.

If you don't want the anxiety that comes from wrong goals, recognize that any goal that can be blocked by other people or circumstances that you have no right or ability to control is not a goal that God wants you to have. And let it go.

I am not saying that you need to abandon building a business that extends God's kingdom or helping children get great results. Those are good things! No, it's just a question of downgrading the significance of those things in our thinking so that they are no longer **goals** upon which our whole sense of who we are depends but are simply **desires**, things we would love to see happen. If they don't, it's disappointing but it's OK.

What would be a good goal for the entrepreneur? How about, being the best possible leader of the people God has given him to lead? A great goal for the school principal would be simply to be the best school principal she can be. That's when her pupils are really going to be helped.

No one else can block those goals. And they are all about character so they are right in line with what God is actually concerned with in your life: what you are **like** rather than what you **do**. God's goal for you is that you become more and more like Jesus in character.

When you align your goals with God's goal, it takes away a lot of anxiety because nobody can block God's goals for your life – difficult people and difficult circumstances can actually help them as you persevere through and grow in character.

The only person who can block God's goal for your life is... you!

2. Cast Your Anxiety Onto God

So we need to humble ourselves before God and then we are to cast all our anxieties onto him.

The principle behind it is that in any situation that is causing you anxiety, you work out prayerfully before God what is your responsibility, what is God's responsibility and what is someone else's responsibility. Then you do what you need to do to fulfil **your** responsibilities.

That might mean forgiving someone. It might mean putting something right – perhaps there's an invoice you've been holding back on paying. It might mean going to speak to someone you realize you've offended.

Once you have done that, you can be sure that you have fulfilled your responsibility and you can confidently say "Over to you, God" and leave everything else with Him. The principle is: **do what is yours to do; then leave the rest to God**.

The Bible is very clear about who is responsible for what. Church leaders often assume that their responsibility is to build their church. Is it? Actually Jesus says quite clearly that it is His responsibility. It's your responsibility to forgive someone who has sinned against you though.

You can cast your anxieties onto God but you can't cast your responsibilities onto Him because He will cast them right back – and you will remain in anxiety. But when you do what is yours to do and then cast onto Him things that really are His responsibility, you really can leave it with Him, confident that he will play his part.

Practise Spiritual Disciplines

If you were to look through the New Testament for a people-system that was not prone to anxiety, you may well come up with the church at Philippi.

In the final chapter, however, we discover that there is some anxiety in Philippi after all: two ladies have fallen out. Paul urges them to agree and in that context he goes on to offer some key exhortations including a command not to be anxious about anything.

In Philippians 4:4–7, Paul lists several essential habits or disciplines we can develop that will help us be anxiety-free disciples and leaders:

- "Rejoice in the Lord always." When you have humbled yourself before God and cast your anxiety upon Him, you can't help but rejoice in His goodness and love for you. As Paul says, "The Lord is at hand" – He is always right there with you. Ultimately – no matter what is going on around you – all is well.
- "Let your reasonableness be known to everyone." Make a habit of being obviously generous and magnanimous.
- In prayer we are to let our requests be known to God. This is the key way to cast your anxieties on to God. When you have fulfilled your responsibility and through prayer placed the rest into the hands of the Creator of the Universe who loves you, wants the best for you, and is right there beside you, why on earth would you worry?
- Give thanks, and keep on giving thanks.
- Then continue with all these until the peace of God comes and guards your heart and mind – which is where the battle takes place. If God's peace isn't guarding your heart and your mind, go round it all one more time. Keep going until you come to a place where you experience that peace.

Choose Your Focus

This is how the passage continues:

Finally, brothers, whatever is true, whatever is honourable, whatever is just, whatever is pure, whatever is lovely, whatever is commendable, if there is any excellence, if there is anything worthy of praise, think [and keep on thinking] about these things. (Philippians 4:8)

Paul is telling us to make a conscious choice about what we focus on. This is not "the power of positive thinking". It is much better than that. We focus on truth.

When you have made a presentation or preached a sermon that you feel didn't go well, the temptation is to feel a failure and to let the anxiety rise up. When you know the truth that you are approved by God, that he is judging you on your character and not on external results, you can use that situation to grow in humility and grace.

Recognize That Conflict In Leadership Is Inevitable

The context for that passage was the danger that personal conflict between two ladies could lead to wider anxiety. Personal conflict is a breeding ground for anxiety. How do we handle conflict?

First, don't be phased by it – realise that it's a normal part of leadership, and indeed life. It's going to happen and it's nothing to be worried about or run away from. What matters is how you handle it.

Choose To Respond Rather Than React

When a potential conflict situation arises, we need to train ourselves not to **react** but to **respond**. In other words, don't rush in with an immediate response but take some time to consider the situation from different angles, perhaps seeking wisdom from others so that your own personal feelings do not cloud your judgement. It takes some determination to choose to do that but it will decrease both your own anxiety and anxiety in your people-system.

Embrace Pain

Many of us have a low threshold for pain and discomfort but the New Testament makes it abundantly clear that we are going to face difficulties of many kinds. Difficulties are not something to be prayed out of the way. We need to embrace pain as something that God uses to develop our character, something that is a necessary part of life and leadership.

We may especially need to raise our threshold for the pain others are experiencing. Their pain can make us anxious. We just want to take it away and we tend to say silly things like, "Don't worry – everything will work out," when we can't possibly know the outcome.

We need to care for those we lead but we are not responsible for them and their problems. Just as God refuses to step in and do things that are our responsibility, we need to refuse to step in to "rescue" them or "medicate" them by making them feel better when it would be better for them to persevere through and become more mature.

It's usually in the most painful times that people and people-systems adapt for the better.

Practical Help

There are some practical things we can do to minimise anxiety.

Rest, eat, and exercise properly. Cutting back on caffeine can help you sleep better and feel calmer.

Take your holidays – I strongly advise a two-week holiday at least once during the year. Don't mix holidays with work.

Respect the Sabbath by setting apart a day each week to honour Him by withdrawing from your work. This is not meant to be the day you catch up with the various projects and activities that we haven't been able to do during the week. Take another day off for those things.

Control your use of smartphones, tablets, and other gadgets – constantly flicking from one thing to another gives you the illusion of multitasking but it actually destroys your ability to concentrate and makes you less effective.

Key Themes For Personal Growth As Leaders

We have emphasized the need to work on our *being* as leaders because our doing flows from our being. As we go through *Freed To Lead* you will notice that this boils down to a few key themes:

1. Know who you are in Christ.
2. Ruthlessly close any doors you've opened to the enemy through past sin and don't open any more.
3. Renew your mind to the truth of Gods Word (which is how you will be transformed).
4. Work from a place of rest.

Rest is particularly important when it comes to personal anxiety. Isaiah tells us that those who wait on the Lord will renew their strength. They will rise up on wings like eagles. We'll look at rest a little more in Session 9.

The leadership dilemma we face when it comes to overcoming personal anxiety is this:

Anxiety always hides or disguises itself so we can be completely unaware of our own anxiety and how it is influencing our leadership. Anxiety also undermines the self-control and renewing of the mind we need to help us overcome it.

As we doggedly choose to put into practice the things we have looked at in this session, we can expect our personal anxiety levels to decrease significantly which will hugely increase our freedom and effectiveness as leaders. Others will have greater confidence in us, we'll see much more clearly how anxiety is at work in the people and people-systems around us, and we'll be in a position to begin to lead our people-system out of anxiety.

SESSION 7:

Overcoming Group Anxiety

LEADER'S NOTES

291

The purpose of this session is to show leaders how anxiety affects people-systems and then give leaders clear, specific strategies for resolving anxiety in their people-systems.

DISCUSSION AIMS

Pause For Thought 1 (page 85)

This Pause For Thought seeks to determine how well people understand the concept of reactivity. Reactivity is one of the most common manifestations of anxiety in any people-system. Of all the issues that we consider in this session, reactivity is most important.

Pause For Thought 2 (page 89)

Our goal in this Pause For Thought is to help people begin to see and understand the work of anxiety in their people-system. One of the greatest failings of leadership is the failure to recognize when anxiety is at work, because anxiety undermines so much of the good that happens in our people-systems.

WORSHIP

- Choose a song about how God upholds us or forgives us; or, choose a song that focuses on God's giving and generosity.
- Read Psalm 37:21–24.
- Pray that your generosity and giving might reflect the generosity and giving of God.
- Thank God for the tokens of His generosity in your life.

Notes for participants are on pages 79–90.

Becoming An Anxiety-Resistant Leader

Dealing with anxiety in your own life is the first and primary step for resolving anxiety in the people-systems that you're part of. We call this "group anxiety" or "systemic anxiety".

Anxiety always escalates when a people-system is overwhelmed by the quantity and speed of information and change.

Anxiety escalates when the institutions and individuals that normally absorb and resolve the anxiety are no longer able to do it.

Anxiety is also empowered by technology.

The anxiety epidemic has given rise to all sorts of technological and managerial attempts to resolve anxiety. These things may help alleviate the symptoms of anxiety, but they will not deal with anxiety itself. In some situations, these things may actually increase anxiety in people.

The only way for people-systems to resist and resolve chronic anxiety is to have anxiety-resistant leaders who are totally committed and connected to their people-system. However, such leaders will themselves often increase anxiety on the way to reducing and resolving anxiety.

Of course, the Bible gives lots of insights into becoming anxiety-resistant leaders. Paul tells us that God has given us a spirit of power and love and self-control. These ingredients are essential to becoming an anxiety-resistant leader.

In addition, Paul tells us to put on the whole armour of God so that we may be able to stand against the schemes of the devil. Anxiety is certainly one of these schemes. And the armour of God might be the only thing that enables us to take our stand.

In putting on the armour of God, we must remember that our struggle is not against flesh and blood. People are not the enemy – and this is especially important to remember when dealing with anxiety in people-systems. Often, the very people we are trying to lead will seem to be our enemies. But they are not.

Paul also reminds us in this passage that we must take a stand and then stand firm. We often resolve a great deal of anxiety by simply taking a principled stand and then holding our ground firmly and gently.

Learning to stand firm begins with having a healthy being grounded in Christ. Knowing who we are in Christ helps us become an anchor for a people-system tossed about by systemic anxiety. But we need to maintain the health of our being if we are to become leaders who help people-systems resolve systemic anxiety.

Five Behaviours Of Anxious People-Systems

Anxiety will pop up in people-systems in some very predictable ways. Friedman, whom we mentioned in session 5, observed five key behaviours in anxious people-systems:

1. Reactivity

2. Herding

3. Blame-shifting

4. Quick-fix mentality

5. Leadership abdication.

Let's take each of these in turn. In our book we discuss these in greater detail. For now, we will briefly describe what they are and then give you some clear strategies for overcoming each one.

Reactivity

The first common behaviour is what we call "reactivity". Whenever you have two or more people or groups of people who get caught up in a cycle of intense and automatic ways of relating to one another, you have discovered reactivity.

Characteristics Of Reactivity

In reactivity, people effectively get stuck in a negative and sinful way of relating to one another. They usually experience really intense emotions – sometimes becoming really volatile. People only seem to focus on what they perceive to be wrong.

They often violate each other's personal boundaries, perhaps by trying to hurt or hinder the other person's relationships. They interfere with one another's communication by interrupting, by speaking over one another, by refusing to listen.

When they are reactive, people will tend to overreact to any perceived hurt, insult, or slight. They will take disagreements far too seriously. And they will engage in ugly personal attacks rather than dealing with legitimate issues. In other words, people are relating to one another out of their flesh instead of a healthy being.

Effects Of Reactivity On People-Systems

Even whole people-systems can get caught up in reactivity. This can happen when two or more primary leaders in the system become reactive towards one another, or it may happen when one people-system starts to be reactive towards another people-system.

When a people-system gets caught up into reactivity, several things happen. First, the people-system begins to focus on self-preservation and stability – even if that hurts the people-system.

Second, reactive systems will try to defend and justify their reactive behaviour. People might disguise their reactivity as some "righteous" cause, like dealing with "false teachers" or protecting the rights of the innocent. Or they will try to make the other person or group look like the bad guy.

Reactive people-systems also lose their resources for dealing with the problems and issues they face. To deal with problems we need resources like objectivity, creativity, time, love, resilience and calmness. We need to think clearly and use our imagination. We need to evaluate our perspectives and expectations. Reactivity causes us to lose all these resources and more.

In the end, if we do not resolve the reactivity of people-systems, they will become demonized and destructive.

Overcoming Reactivity

We can't assume that if we ignore reactivity then it will go away. That just increases reactivity. Trying to hide or disguise reactivity also increases it. But there are ways to disarm reactivity. We begin by exercising self-control, especially as leaders. We must refuse to become reactive ourselves.

If we expose it, calling it what it is, we can often overcome it.

If we persist in giving grace to one another just as God in Christ has given grace to us, then we can disarm reactivity. Grace is a powerful force for removing reactivity. It's very difficult to maintain reactivity in the face of grace.

We need to carefully identify and evaluate perceptions – our own and others'. Many times people get caught up in reactivity because they have the wrong perceptions about something. Remember how anxiety distorts everything. This includes our perceptions.

We must learn how to respond thoughtfully with gentle firmness. This means that we need to step back, take a deep breath, and make a good choice. This also means that we must take a stand.

We need to focus on health and healthy ways of doing things in our people-system. So often we get stuck in reactivity by focusing on what is wrong and what is **unhealthy**. We keep trying to fix it – but this only creates more anxiety. However, when we focus on what is **healthy** and seek to maintain healthy ways of doing things, we will create a sense of hope.

Dealing with reactivity requires that we learn how to move in the opposite spirit: where there is bitterness, we show forgiveness; where there is anger, we express calm; where there is criticism, we express appreciation.

Finally, we must remember the words of Paul to Timothy: 2 Timothy 2:24–26. If we refuse to argue with others, we disarm reactivity and also give God room to speak to people's hearts and expose their wrongdoing so they might repent.

Herding

The next behaviour is what we call "herding". It's like the behaviour of animals when they feel under threat.

Characteristics Of Herding

When people in a people-system begin to experience a lot of anxiety they tend to bunch together in a way that does not allow people to take responsibility and act maturely. They insist that everyone in the people-system bunch up and stick together no matter what. People might say, "Can't we all just get along. We need to forget our differences for the common good."

Then, everybody starts to conform to or give in to the least mature, most dependent, or most dysfunctional members in the people-system. When the people-system is herding, the people who are the most dysfunctional tend to be the ones who are in control.

Overcoming Herding

In order to overcome herding, we must focus on the **mature** people in the system. They are the ones who can help resolve anxiety. Our goal is to promote maturity throughout the system. We also need to emphasize the strengths of our people and our system and then use them to overcome the herding.

It's essential that we encourage integrity and maturity in people. Mature people will be able to take personal responsibility and resist the power of herding. They will help others do the same.

As leaders we must be emotionally open and available to people. We cannot close ourselves off. But it's also important that we take clear, principled stands on issues while we remain fully connected to the people around us.

Blame-Shifting

The third behaviour is called blame-shifting. When people focus on forces that they believe have victimized or oppressed them rather than taking personal responsibility for their lives, they have succumbed to blame-shifting.

We see blame-shifting at work every day, as various groups persistently blame others for the problems in the world. Blame-shifting never resolves an issue; it just leads to anger, frustration and hopelessness.

Overcoming Blame-Shifting

Several strategies will help us overcome blame-shifting. We need to reframe the issues we're dealing with in terms of our people-systems.

Second, as before we must focus on developing maturity and mature people in our people-systems. Maturity helps us overcome those things that produce anxiety.

We must also review our perceptions and expectations, making sure that we examine and evaluate them very carefully.

When we experience challenges to our people-systems, we must describe them and choose our response to them in terms of the healthy aspects of our people-systems.

Finally, as leaders we must encourage people to take appropriate responsibility for themselves by modelling what it means to take appropriate responsibility. When people see it in us, they will be more likely to do it themselves.

Quick-Fix Mentality

The fourth behaviour of an anxious people-system comes from our tendency to avoid anything that is painful or uncomfortable. Anxious people want to avoid anything that might be painful or unpleasant. So when pain or difficulty comes, most people want quick relief from it. And they'll do anything to get it. We call this the "quick-fix mentality".

In the quick-fix mentality, if the government introduces some painful policies, we'll replace the government with one that makes us feel better rather than follow the policies – no matter how good they might be.

Overcoming Quick-Fix Mentality

Many people and people-systems fail to recognize that becoming healthy and mature is a process that takes time.

In order to overcome the quick-fix mentality, we must embrace pain and difficulty.

As leaders, we must work very, very hard to encourage, allow, and defend time and space for processes to mature. We must ensure that people do not try to rush the soufflé.

We must also expose any idealistic distortions. And there are a lot of them!

One of the most common distortions is the assumption that people in churches should never have conflict with one another.

Another idealistic distortion is that maturity can happen quickly. Or that we can fix big problems with little effort.

In order to help our people-system resist the urge for quick fixes we need to establish some clear, realistic "signposts" that show people that progress is happening.

If we want to overcome the quick-fix mentality then we must calmly and steadily press on.

Leadership Abdication

The final behaviour for people-systems caught up in anxiety is what we call "leadership abdication". If this happens then we allow the behaviours we've looked at to shape us rather than us shaping them.

If we abdicate our responsibilities as leaders then there is really no hope for our people-systems to overcome anxiety. There is really no hope for our people-systems to achieve their God-given destiny.

Overcoming Leadership Abdication

As leaders, we must exercise self-control and steadfastness. We have to remember that self-control is the only biblical form of control and it's a fruit of the Holy Spirit.

As leaders, we need to seek our own maturity and integrity. One of the greatest gifts that we can give to our people-system, whether it's a marketplace system or a church, is **ourselves** as mature leaders.

If we are mature as a leader, then we will naturally help other people become mature. We will also attract more mature people to ourselves.

The more mature people we have around us, the more likely it is that our people-system will become mature.

As Christian leaders, we need to walk by the Spirit of God. This means allowing the Holy Spirit to lead us in our decision-making. This also means allowing the Holy Spirit to produce the fruit of the Spirit inside of us.

In order to overcome leadership abdication, we must embrace the responsibilities of leadership. We must recognize that leadership costs a lot and it's not easy. We have to accept the consequences of our decisions.

Not only must we embrace our responsibilities, but we must also commit to persevere in our leadership. We cannot expect great things to happen in a few weeks. Making significant change and resolving major issues may take many years. We must never give up, never surrender. Perseverance is one major indicator of our love for our people.

This may actually require us to put the symbolic stake in the ground.

Leading People-Systems Out Of Anxiety

Overall, Christians who become effective leaders of people-systems take responsibility for themselves so they become anxiety-resistant leaders. They resist the tyranny of the seemingly urgent in order to focus on the healthy processes that may require time and patience but also lead to lasting results.

These leaders expect relentless resistance, opposition, and sabotage, knowing that the people who need them the most will often be the people who seek to undermine them.

They submit to God and resist the devil, not only in their own lives but also in their people-systems.

Instead of allowing anxiety to shape them, these leaders seek to shape the mindsets of their people with faith, hope, and love.

But this leads us to our leadership dilemma. True, healthy, connected leaders are the only hope for resolving anxiety in any system.

True leaders will become lightning rods for systemic anxiety, which is essential for draining away the power of anxiety. But this demands that we are appropriately "grounded" (or "earthed") in Jesus.

As anyone knows, lightning would destroy an ungrounded (unearthed) lightning rod. In the same way, if you are not grounded in Jesus as a leader, then the anxiety of your people-system will burn you out.

Authentic, healthy, connected leaders are the only hope for resolving anxiety in any people-system. But chronically anxious people-systems will always try to eliminate healthy leaders from the system before anxiety is resolved.

This is one reason why businesses, governments, and churches all over the world are seeing such rapid turnover in leadership.

In a sense, this is good news. If the chronically anxious people-system might fire you no matter what you do, then you might as well choose to lead!

SESSION 8:

Building And Keeping Trust

LEADER'S NOTES

303

The purpose of this session is to introduce leaders to the concept of trust and how trust influences everything in their leadership. The session will show leaders how to build trust as well as how to restore trust when it is broken.

DISCUSSION AIMS

Pause For Thought 1 (page 94)

In this Pause For Thought, we want people to begin wrestling with the issue of trust. All people place a very high value on trust, but few people really consider what trust is all about until their trust has been violated. The problem then is that many people will consequently define their understanding of trust based on the violation of trust instead of on a healthy definition of trust.

Pause For Thought 2 (page 103)

The goal of this Pause For Thought is to help leaders determine how to improve their credibility so that others might trust them more. We begin by reinforcing (with the first two questions) how beneficial trust really is in any person or people-system.

WORSHIP

- Choose a song about God's justice or about how God will never leave or forsake us.
- Read Psalm 37:25–28.
- Thank God for your physical or spiritual children and the promise that they shall become a blessing.

Notes for participants are on pages 91–104.

Trust

What can you trust? More importantly whom can you trust? And more importantly still, can people trust you? Do they trust you?

Paul says in 1 Corinthians 4:2, "It is required of stewards [leaders] that they be found trustworthy."

Why? Lack of trust in a leader is a disaster. You are never going to be able to lead effectively unless you can change that.

Indicators Of A Low Trust People-System

It doesn't just depend on you. You may be leading in a people-system with a low-trust environment. How can you tell?

Atmosphere Of Suspicion

There will be an atmosphere of suspicion so there will be things like: manipulated or distorted facts and "spinning" the truth; people withholding information; a lot of blaming, criticizing and accusations flying about; and the biggest clue, secrets, and secret meetings.

Atmosphere Of Anxiety

There will also be a great deal of anxiety: people won't be willing to take risks, mistakes will be covered up, and there will be a lot of overpromising and underdelivering.

Atmosphere Of Tension And Friction

Finally there will be an environment of tension and friction; people trying hard to get personal credit; open resistance to new ideas and change; and unrealistic expectations.

In a low trust people-system, you are forever treading on egg shells and watching your back. It isn't much fun being a leader in that kind of environment!

Indicators Of A High Trust People-System

So what does a people-system with a high level of trust look like?

Atmosphere Of Openness

There will be an environment of openness where information is shared openly, mistakes are tolerated and even encouraged, people will be vulnerable and real, and there will be genuine accountability.

Atmosphere Of Honour

People will be honoured. The focus will be on others rather than on ourselves. People will share credit, they will be honest, they will be loyal to those who aren't present, and will be happy to collaborate and co-operate with each other.

Atmosphere Of Creativity

And in a high trust people-system you'll find a great deal of creative energy and vitality, reduced anxiety, good teamwork, increased innovation, and better communication.

A low-trust people-system is in many ways like the legalistic Pharisaical system in which people comply with the letter of the law because they have to. Their heart is not in it so it's not much fun and it's not rewarding.

In a high-trust environment on the other hand, people are trusted to do what they think is right. They are given freedom to use their initiative – freedom to fail in effect. When you get high levels of trust, you are talking about a system based on grace.

The Atmosphere Of Trust That God Creates

One of the most significant things you can do as a leader is make sure you yourself have a deep understanding of the grace of God. Then simply come to your people the same way He comes to you.

That's a great principle for most aspects of leadership. Look how God trusts us:

1. God gives us a huge commission – to go into all the world and make disciples – and gives us the means to fulfil it.

2. Having delegated it to us, He trusts us to get on with it. We are quite literally the Body of Christ, called to do His work. There is no plan B – yet God confidently predicts in Revelation 19:7 that the Bride will have made herself ready for Christ's return. What amazing trust He expresses in us!

3. All the while He gives us freedom to fail.

Failure is nothing to be frightened of incidentally. On the contrary, healthy failure can increase trust in a people-system.

If someone fails and you explode at them, blame them, cover the failure up, give up or back away from them, trust will be eroded. But if you evaluate failures openly, encouraging responsibility and learning without casting blame, trust will grow.

4. When we go wrong, God disciplines. It is done out of love.

5. God is always available.

6. God shows unswerving loyalty to us even when we are disloyal to Him.

7. God is slow to anger and abounding in steadfast love.

If we can understand that and simply act the same way, we won't go far wrong.

Building Trust

What is trust? All trust flows from two dynamics, our old friends **being** (integrity, character) and **doing** (skills, good track record).

Our definition of trust is "to place your confidence in the being and doing of another".

You could express it as an equation: $QB + QD = C$. That is, Quality of *Being* + Quality of *Doing* = Amount of *Confidence*. If people feel your being is right and that you are competent to do, they will trust you and follow you.

Now we see why God is the ultimate model for trust. His **being** is pure love. He never changes. He can **do** anything and He always does what He promises.

A good leader will act as a lightning rod to drain away anxiety and mistrust from their people-system. When mistrust hits, it drains away into the ground through the leader.

The Apostle Paul faced a low trust environment in the church in Corinth. His authority had been undermined by an influential teacher who was misleading the people. The church clearly had the suspicion, fear, and tension that indicates a people-system with low levels of trust. Paul had visited them but encountered open resistance so he wrote them what he calls a distressing letter. Many repented as a result but a small group was still being openly critical of him. Difficult situation. In 2 Corinthians, Paul is hoping to bring them out of a low-trust environment and start trusting him again. Let's see how he goes about it.

He starts chapter 3 by saying, "Are we beginning to commend ourselves again? Or do we need, as some do, letters of recommendation to you, or from you?" to which the obvious answer is "no".

So here are two things that Paul **didn't** do to get people to trust him. He didn't try to commend himself – and he didn't try to get others to commend him. Because trust is a function of being and doing, not fine words.

Later in the same letter (5:11–12) he says:

What we are is known to God, and I hope it is known also to your conscience. We are not commending ourselves to you again but giving you cause to boast about us, so that you may be able to answer those who boast about outward appearance and not about what is in the heart.

He is saying, "I don't need to commend myself. I hope by now you know who I am – my being, my heart." As leaders who want to be trusted, our being – our character – is of supreme importance. People will eventually see it for what it is, whether that's positive or negative. I can't give you any tips on your being apart from saying, keep walking with God and you will become more and more like Jesus.

Trust-Building Behaviours Of Being (Character)

As your character becomes more and more like Jesus, you will automatically exhibit behaviours like His that will cause people to trust you because the behaviours show them that your being is good. We call these things "trust-building behaviours of being". You will:

- Speak the truth in love.
- Show respect and honour.
- Model transparency. Let your yes be yes and your no, no. Just be who you are. Never present yourself as something you're not.
- Right wrongs.
- Show loyalty even to people who are being disloyal to you.
- Pay attention to others.
- Exercise self-control, the final item in the list of the fruit of the Spirit.
- Express gratitude.
- Give grace to others.

There is a list of these trust-building behaviours of being in your Participant's Guide (on pages 98–99). But you can't just look at the list and decide to use these behaviours as if they were techniques you can learn. If they don't genuinely come from your being, people will see right through them.

Trust-Building Behaviours Of Doing (Competence)

Trust is about being **and** doing. If you have the best being in the world, people will love you but they won't necessarily follow you, especially in a low-trust environment. Paul's letter to the Corinthians continues with Paul saying in chapter 3 that God has made him "competent" to be a minister. He wants them to see that he not only has a good being but he is also capable of **doing** the job of leading them well.

The people you lead need to know not only that your being is good but that you are also **competent** to lead them. In other words, they need to know that your **doing** is good too.

When you use your abilities, skills and strengths well – your doing – people will see your competence, your capability. Another word we could use is "credibility". Part of it is your track record: whether or not you deliver results, whether or not you have a history of getting the system to where you were intending to lead it. Part of it is whether people judge you capable of leading them into the future.

There are some things that you can consciously choose to do in order to demonstrate that your doing is good. We call these trust-building behaviours of doing. These are things like:

- Deliver results – don't make excuses.
- Get better – continually improve on what you do. Never be satisfied with where you are. Make small changes to keep improving.
- Confront reality.
- Clarify expectations.
- Practise genuine accountability.

- Listen actively – make the person you are speaking to feel they are the only one in the universe.
- Keep commitments.
- Extend trust to others. There's nothing like trusting others if you want them to trust you.
- Do what you can to meet the needs of followers to enable them to do what they have to do.

Losing And Regaining Trust

These trust-building behaviours of doing are particularly helpful if you find yourself in a situation where you need to build or rebuild trust as we'll see in a moment. First, let's understand the function of time in losing and regaining trust.

Trust takes a long time to build. That is the nature of trust: it takes time to build but can be lost in an instant.

The quickest way to destroy trust is for your behaviour to cause people to doubt your being – your integrity, your good will. That will happen if you violate a trust-building behaviour of being. They may overlook one or even two failings – they don't expect you to be perfect – but if they perceive that it is happening consistently, people will lose their trust in you because they will doubt your being.

If you want to rebuild trust, first of all, of course, you have to stop violating the trust-building behaviours of being. But that is not necessarily enough.

The quickest way to increase trust is through trust-building behaviours of doing.

What we're not saying here, however, is that in order to rebuild trust, you can go on a course and learn how to do some of those trust-building behaviours of doing. Your doing always flows from your being. You cannot simply turn on your doing – at least not consistently – if your being is not right.

It will be helpful to you to bear the behaviours of doing in mind and actively try to use them in order to increase people's trust. But you can't fake it. You could read a book to learn how to practise accountability but when push comes to shove it's not just knowing how to be accountable that matters, it's actually putting it into practice. You can't do these behaviours of doing consistently unless your being is healthy.

Interestingly, violating behaviours of doing doesn't decrease trust in the same way as violating behaviours of being. For example, if someone comes up to speak to me and I'm trying to get ready for a meeting and fail to practise active listening, I've violated a behaviour of doing. But if I've shown them respect in the past and they've seen me consistently pay attention to others, if I'm not rude or dismissive to them, and if I transparently say, "I'm sorry but I'm really distracted at the moment and I'm not giving you the attention that I would like," then my failure to listen actively to that person would probably not decrease their trust in me. That brings us to our leadership dilemma:

People-systems can't function without trust. But they are increasingly prone to anxiety which degrades trust. Increasingly society itself is a low-trust environment with people actively trying to destroy trust in leaders. The end result is that there is a corrosive pessimism towards leaders and people-systems.

However, a leader who is well connected to their people-system yet doesn't react to all this acts as a lightning rod to drain anxiety from the people-system and enable people to trust.

It all starts with your being, your character, knowing who you are in Christ, and working to become more and more like Jesus. That then works out through your doing, your God-given competence to be the person He has called you to be in the leadership role He has called you to.

He has chosen you as a leader and placed you where you are. In Christ you have the capacity to become someone whom people trust implicitly.

SESSION 9:

Overcoming Personal Pitfalls

LEADER'S NOTES

313

The purpose of this session is to help participants work out strategies to overcome some common personal pitfalls that affect leaders.

DISCUSSION AIMS

Pause For Thought 1 (page 108)

Our hope in this Pause For Thought is that people in your group will identify the challenges and temptations that they face as leaders in order to gain the courage and determination to overcome these challenges and temptations. It is essential that people understand that the presence of challenges and temptations means that they are being effective as leaders not that they are being ineffective as leaders. Too many people live with the idealistic distortion that if we were really good leaders then leadership would be easy.

Pause For Thought 2 (page 115)

We often find that if people identify their weaknesses, temptations and pitfall susceptibilities, then they will have an easier time overcoming these. It is when people feel unable to own up to these things that they often become victims of them. This Pause For Thought seeks to help people identify these issues in their lives so that they might develop a plan for overcoming them.

WORSHIP

- Choose a song that praises God for His righteousness and wisdom.
- Read Psalm 37:29–31.
- Surrender yourselves to God anew and ask God to put His will in your hearts.

Notes for participants are on pages 105–116.

Types Of Personal Leadership Pitfall

In this session we are going to look at various personal pitfalls we face. There are a lot of them! We're going to look at personal pitfalls in the areas of temptation, self-centredness, emotions, communication, and exhaustion.

Temptation Pitfalls

All temptation is simply an attempt to get you to meet your legitimate needs for significance, security, and acceptance independently of God. It's not wrong to want to feel significant, secure, and accepted, but actually you could not possibly become more significant, secure, and accepted than you already are in Christ. Will you trust God to meet your deepest needs or will you look to something else?

Richard Foster identifies money, sex, and power as the greatest temptations of our age and those are probably the top three for most of us in leadership positions.

Money

How well do we manage our personal finances? Are we prone to greed? How generous is our giving?

Do we insist on fiscal accountability for our people-system or our church but don't show the same responsibility with our own personal finances?

We may have a lot of discretion over how our organisation's or department's funds are used. It's so easy to start playing things to our own advantage – quite possibly legitimately as far as the rules go but nevertheless perhaps not quite in a godly way. Would you sign off your own expenses if they were someone else's?

Sex

It's very easy to fall into fantasy and daydreaming about that attractive person in the workplace. Jesus was clear that lust is the same sin as adultery. We need to recognize that it's the start of a slippery slope – and don't think it couldn't happen to you. We're all vulnerable.

Pornography is one of the greatest evils in our world today and very many leaders are stuck in it. Surely it can't affect my leadership? Oh yes it can – having a big door like that open to the enemy means that your being is not healthy. It will work out in your doing. People will instinctively sense that things aren't right even if they don't know exactly what the problem is.

But don't think you can't get out of an addictive sin like that. Paul says in Romans 6 that the power of sin is broken in your life if you are a Christian. That is the truth whether it feels true or not. *The Freedom In Christ Discipleship Course* has more on that.

Power

As a leader, you're in charge – it's all too easy to forget that you are there to serve and start behaving in a dominant way. It's easy too to abuse the power of being a leader by being manipulative. Say the right things and you can manipulate people in your team very easily.

If you recognize in yourself a temptation to control or manipulate people and situations, or to make sure others know your job title and give you the respect you feel you are due, ask yourself why. It probably means you are not yet as secure as you could be in who you are in Christ.

Avoiding Temptation Pitfalls

In 1 Corinthians 10:13 God promises to provide a way of escape from every temptation. Where is it? Right at the start of the process, when the tempting thought first comes into your mind.

Your mind is like an airport and you are the air traffic controller. A lot of tempting thoughts ask for permission to land. But you have complete control over which will land and which will be turned away. You have to decide right at the outset, however. The moment you give a tempting thought permission to land, the chances of your being able to turn it away reduce significantly.

The answer? To reject the tempting thought as soon as it appears because you have learned to recognize what's really going on. We need to learn to be relentlessly honest with ourselves.

Self-Centredness Pitfalls

Then we have self-centredness pitfalls – this is when we make things "all about me".

Messiah

We can develop a "Messiah complex" where we get our sense of who we are by kidding ourselves that we are the saviour of our people-system, that they just couldn't survive without us. None of us is indispensable and if we start thinking we are, God might just have to show us clearly that we're not.

Martyr

Somewhat similar but expressed in a different way is the "martyr complex". This is where we use self-sacrifice and suffering to kid ourselves that we are indispensable. "I will carry the cross and sacrifice everything for these people!" We feel the need to put everyone else's needs above our own – "no one else will do it, poor old me" – and genuinely feel that we are the only one who cares.

The people you lead will try to show you that they really do care by over-compensating. But it's never enough. The martyr just doesn't see it and the followers eventually reach the end of their tether and give up.

Hermit

Or we can be hermits who sit back, let our team run ahead and watch them... as they run off the edge of a cliff. If you tend towards passivity, it's probably down to cowardice, a fear of what people might think or say.

Emotional Pitfalls

Let's turn now to emotional pitfalls.

Bitterness

This is a huge issue – any unforgiveness in you opens a big wide door to the enemy to come marching into your life. A leader who has not learnt to forgive relentlessly is heading for big trouble. If there is a lot of pain from an unhealthy people-system, this will be a daily struggle. You just need to grit your teeth and keep affirming your forgiveness for whoever it is and keep praying blessing on them. The key point, of course, is that it's for your own freedom that Jesus commands you to forgive.

Anger

Then there's anger along with resentment and frustration. If you show these things you will alienate people and destroy your credibility. When we express anger we arrogantly turn the recipient of our anger into the underdog.

We looked in a previous session at how an **uncertain** goal can be a cause of anxiety. Well, if you find you are getting angry a lot, it might well be an indication that you have a goal that you feel is being **blocked**. The remedy is the same: take a look at your goals and check that they are in line with God's goals, if necessary downgrading them to "nice to haves" but not essential to your personal sense of success or who you are.

Defensiveness

In Christ you don't ever need to defend yourself. If you are wrong, you don't have a defence. If you are right, you don't need a defence because God Himself will defend you. We can learn to be open and emotionally available to our people and they will love us for it.

Communication Pitfalls

It's important to understand that communication is fundamentally an **emotional** rather than an intellectual process. There is much more to it than simply the factual information that words might convey. It matters a great deal who is saying the words, how they are saying them and what the hearer feels about that person. Body language says a whole lot more than the words themselves. That's why humour can really help communication – it engages emotional processes.

It's also why close communication – a face to face chat – is much better than distant communication, a letter or an email. The greater the **distance** from the person you're communicating with, the greater the sense of "safety" and the greater the tendency to abandon self-control and personal responsibility.

In my experience most people choose to raise difficult issues by email because the distance makes it feel easier. I have learned by bitter experience not to respond in the same way but to discuss the issues face-to-face. You have a much greater chance of resolving them that way.

Pursuit Behaviours

People want to make a connection with leaders and if they feel they haven't made a connection with you in a normal, healthy way, they will sometimes come after you in an inappropriate way – and these things are called "pursuit behaviours".

They may criticize you. If you turn away, it can escalate quickly into bitterness and recrimination. Most churches have wounded people who are harsh and bitter and won't let people in, yet paradoxically they long to let people in.

Or they may always be trying to rescue you, to be indispensable to you. They don't like to think that you can live without them. This is a big one for pastors.

It's easy to mistake these pursuit behaviours for personal attack or rebellion. They make you want to turn away but actually it's much better to engage with those who pursue you. Allow yourself to be "caught". Stop, open yourself up, listen actively to what they are saying and respond thoughtfully. You may be able to lead them into a more mature pattern of behaviour. They are not out to get you – they just want to connect with you.

Mind you, on the other hand... there probably are some people who really are out to get you!

Exhaustion Pitfalls

And finally we come to exhaustion pitfalls. All of us have a lot to do most of the time. When God created the world he worked for six days and rested on the seventh. But Adam was created on the sixth day. For him it was just the opposite. He rested and had fellowship with God the first day of his life and **then** worked. That's how it's meant to be for us. We work from a place of rest. We don't work and then collapse into rest to recover.

And yet, it seems to go with the territory that leaders get tired. When we do, it leaves us vulnerable to blow-out, bankruptcy, and burnout.

Blow-out is giving into temptation because your defences are down. Before you know it you can hit **bankruptcy** where you don't have anything fresh to offer. And if that continues, over time it will lead us to **burnout**: physical, emotional, mental, and spiritual exhaustion.

Avoiding Exhaustion Pitfalls

We get tired because we want to do well in our leading. We want to bear fruit. We are deceived into thinking that it's down to our own strenuous efforts, but that's a fatal flaw in our belief system.

Jesus wants us to bear fruit even more than we do ourselves. But interestingly He never, ever commanded us to bear fruit. In John 15:4, He gave us a different command:

"Abide in me, and I in you. As the branch cannot bear fruit by itself, unless it abides in the vine, neither can you, unless you abide in me."

A branch on a vine doesn't strain in order to get grapes to pop out. It just hangs around connected to the main plant and one day suddenly there is the fruit. It just happens naturally at the right time.

The big principle that many Christian leaders never fully appreciate other than as a theological principle is, you will bear fruit only if you are genuinely connected to Jesus, if you are working from a place of internal rest.

There's a fascinating insight in Hebrews 4:

*So then, there remains a Sabbath rest for the people of God, for whoever has entered God's rest has also rested from his works as God did from his. Let us therefore **strive** to enter that rest, so that no one may fall by the same sort of disobedience.*

Hebrews 4:9–11

We are commanded to strive... in order to enter God's rest! It seems a contradiction in terms. But it's hard work to get to the place where we are leading out of a position of rest, from our being. We need to renew our minds so that we really understand that there will be no lasting fruit unless it is from a place of resting in Christ. And that takes time and effort.

Then we will constantly need to keep reminding ourselves of that key truth.

Regular **prayer and Bible reading** will help hugely. When you take time to pray, you connect with the reality of God and realize how much bigger he is than anything else going on in your life. When you read his word, you are connecting with pure, unadulterated truth that will explode the lies that the world, the flesh, and the devil constantly throw your way.

Take time out to seek God and His will for your life. I take a day out a month. I know that's not practical for everyone but you could take a weekend or even a week once a year.

Use *The Steps To Freedom In Christ* on an annual basis. I do it personally with one or two spiritual heavyweights and ask them to give me a hard time. It's amazing how much rubbish I can pick up in a year.

Get a close accountability relationship where you are regularly challenged to be vulnerable and honest.

Avoiding Personal Pitfalls

Paul says in Romans 13:14, "Put on the Lord Jesus Christ, and make no provision for the flesh, to gratify its desires." When it comes to avoiding personal pitfalls in Christian leadership, one of the most helpful things you can do is keep reminding yourself just how damaging it is to you personally and to the organization you lead, if you allow the enemy to get a foothold – a base of operations – in your life.

Don't be deceived into thinking you can handle it or maintain it as it is or that sin is not that serious. Unresolved sin will always lead you further and further away from God and damage you as a leader.

The leadership dilemma for this session is short:

We have everything we need in Christ to avoid these pitfalls, but even so, if we are not very careful, we will tend to keep falling into them.

Let me remind you of the four key principles for our personal lives as leaders:

1. Know who you are in Christ.
2. Ruthlessly close any doors you've opened to the enemy through past sin and don't open any more.
3. Renew your mind to the truth of God's Word (which is how you will be transformed).
4. Work from a place of rest.

As you focus on these principles and put them into practice, I am confident that you will be not just an authentic Christian leader but a great Christian leader, one who will bear fruit that will last for eternity. Go for it!

Overcoming Group Pitfalls

The purpose of this session is to help participants identify some common group or "systemic" pitfalls that affect leaders and people-systems and give them strategies to overcome them.

DISCUSSION AIMS

Pause For Thought 1 (page 124)

In this Pause For Thought, we want people to see how they might have contributed to group pitfalls in the past so that they might choose not to do it again in the future. We also want people to be encouraged that the presence of group pitfalls indicates that their leadership is having a positive effect on their people-system.

Pause For Thought 2 (page 126)

In this Pause For Thought, it is important to ensure that people really understand the fallacy of the belief that, if we only have expertise, empathy, togetherness, or position then we will necessarily become better leaders. The two most common leadership delusions are the delusion of expertise and the delusion of empathy.

WORSHIP

- Choose a song that celebrates the promises of God and their fulfilment in our lives.
- Read Psalm 37:32–36.
- Surrender any difficult situations or relationships you have to God, asking for His deliverance.
- Thank God that He will not abandon you, that God will be your defender.

Notes for participants are on pages 117–128.

Group Pitfalls

Our effective leadership will always trigger a number of predictable reactions among the people we lead. These situations indicate that our leadership is being effective, not that we are poor leaders.

We call these situations or reactions "group pitfalls" or "systemic pitfalls". The key thing to remember is this: It's not these situations by themselves that are the pitfalls, but our wrong reactions or responses to these situations!

We need to remember that a certain degree of conflict and uncertainty will always occur in any people-system. The point is that we don't have to allow these things to lead us into wrong or inappropriate behaviours as leaders – thus falling into the pitfalls. So when we talk about "pitfalls" here, we are not talking only about the things themselves but also how we respond to these things as leaders.

These pitfalls happen because people simply don't like change and they are instinctively afraid of what they might lose. This means they naturally resist good leadership – even when they suspect the leadership may lead to good outcomes – because good leadership always brings about change.

If we react or respond to these pitfalls inappropriately, then we'll create anxiety and instability in our people-system and undermine our leadership. Our unhealthy reaction to these pitfalls will actually make them worse. So we need to learn to avoid or deal with these pitfalls effectively.

Dilemmas Not Problems

These pitfalls are dilemmas, not problems. It's essential that we understand the difference.

Problems are issues that can be solved and resolved.

Dilemmas are issues that by their nature cannot be solved. There are no easy solutions. The best we can do is try to manage dilemmas while they work themselves out.

The point is this: when we have a dilemma, by definition there are no easy answers. People-system pitfalls are dilemmas that require time, patience, and creativity to work through.

Four Common Group Pitfalls

There are four common pitfalls when it comes to people-systems: selfishness, sabotage, strife, and suffering.

Selfishness

Ironically, selfishness will often pop up when a people-system is getting healthier. As a people-system becomes stronger, people who have sacrificed or suffered for the sake of the people-system often want to get the benefits they feel they deserve. This may lead them to become selfish.

Selfishness is an inappropriate focus on yourself – being self-centred, self-seeking, or self-referential. At its heart, it's the refusal to take appropriate personal responsibility for your character or your perceived needs. It's a form of immaturity. Immature people will always demand that other people give in to or adjust to their problems or demands.

One challenge for us is mistaking immaturity for rebellion. Initially, they may look very similar. However, immaturity is a **dilemma** that people must work through as they become mature, while rebellion is a sin problem that requires repentance. If we treat immature people as if they are rebellious, then they will become rebellious – creating an even bigger dilemma!

To avoid the pitfall of selfishness, we must **model healthy self-giving** as a leader. One of the greatest dangers we face as leaders is becoming selfish ourselves. We need to **promote maturity by being mature** ourselves, taking responsibility for our mind, will, and emotions. As difficult as it might be, we need to **focus on developing healthy and mature people** in our people-system, without giving in to selfishness.

Sabotage

The second common pitfall for people-systems is sabotage. Sabotage is seeking to destroy, damage, obstruct, or hinder leaders or change, sometimes for personal or political advantage.

Sometimes people will sabotage leaders because there are shifting relationships in the people-system.

People may also sabotage leaders because of their own flesh, that sinful aspect of our humanity. When some people don't get their own way, they will make sure that no one else succeeds either. Or, our pride may make us think we are right and others are wrong, so we sabotage their efforts in order to get our own way.

Occasionally, sabotage may be demonically inspired. Satan can whisper thoughts into people's minds that, left unchecked, may lead them to sabotage something. As Paul says in 2 Corinthians 2, we don't want to be ignorant of Satan's schemes.

There are a number of common ways that sabotage manifests itself:

- Spreading discontent
- Magnifying the potential loss of doing something
- Misrepresenting a leader or a decision
- Passive aggressive behaviour
- Changing your mind after the group has made a decision
- Putting in extra conditions on an agreement late in negotiations or even after negotiations have been completed

- Agreeing publicly while undermining something privately
- Spreading gossip and rumours
- Bullying and intimidation.

As leaders, we must ensure that our being is fully grounded in Jesus Christ so that we can respond calmly, peacefully, and intentionally to sabotage. Most of the time sabotage is successful because we allow it to create anxiety in us and our people-system. To work through sabotage, we must focus on building healthy people and healthy ways of doing things in our people-system.

Strife

The third common pitfall for people-systems is strife. Strife is just another word for friction and conflict. Basically, strife describes problems within interpersonal relationships. It's important to remember that strife will often increase as people are learning to become mature. In that sense, we cannot avoid strife. But we must learn how to work through it in a healthy manner.

Some things we tend to do never work when it comes to strife. Trying to explain or justify our position won't help. Defending ourselves makes things worse. If we withdraw and refuse to engage in the conflict then it just gets worse. Blaming someone else or something else for the problem never works. Trying to placate or appease the other person just makes the conflict worse. Bargaining with the person or appealing to fairness doesn't work either. All these common responses will ultimately increase rather than resolve strife.

As a leader, we must ensure that our being is grounded in Christ so that we don't try to avoid strife. If we allow strife to create anxiety in us as leaders, then strife will create anxiety in our people-system.

Instead, we need to encourage people to work through strife with love, mercy and grace. People need to understand that strife is normal and working through strife can actually promote health in a people-system. We need to model appropriate responses to strife.

As a leader, we can help people gain new, healthier perspectives on strife. For example, we might help people understand that strife is one way that God forms our character as people.

Suffering

The final people-system pitfall, suffering, is essentially the collective effect of all the other pitfalls. Suffering is experiencing something that we perceive to be negative or unpleasant. However, simply because something is negative or unpleasant doesn't necessarily make that thing bad. Pain, for example, is a natural part of our growth and development. If we could not feel pain, then we would not be healthy.

We need to understand that various difficulties will always accompany a people-system that has effective leadership. Our willingness and ability as leaders to embrace suffering will determine the willingness and ability of the people-system we lead to embrace suffering. Suffering is one of the things the Bible promises we will experience as Christians, so it's important as leaders that we help our people go through suffering well.

Overcoming Group Pitfalls

As leaders, we can avoid these group pitfalls. To do so, we must **lead from our identity fully grounded in Christ** while maintaining a calm leadership presence.

It's essential that we **seek fresh and different perspectives** on what's happening in our people-system.

As a leader, we can **welcome conflict** as normal and as an opportunity for growth. Just as the human immune system becomes healthier as it fights off various diseases, so a people-system will become healthier as it goes through various struggles. This means that we need to **embrace suffering** as part of our calling in leadership.

In order to avoid falling into these pits, we must **resist idealistic distortions and expectations**. Sometimes we set such lofty, idealistic expectations for what life in church or the workplace should be like that we miss the importance of what is happening around us.

Leadership Delusions

Not only are there common pitfalls that we must avoid, but there are also four common delusions that we experience as leaders. A delusion is a false belief or impression we maintain even when it's contradicted by reality. The delusion is that these things will by themselves make us better leaders. More often than not, these delusions may undermine our effectiveness as leaders.

The Delusion Of Expertise

The delusion of expertise is the fallacy that if we only have the right knowledge or the right techniques then we will be effective leaders. In this delusion, we believe that successful leadership involves overcoming a series of problems for which there are clear-cut solutions provided by the right knowledge or the right technique. Often, the solutions we seek involve some kind of new technology.

This delusion also includes the false belief that if something succeeds in one people-system then it will succeed in another similar people-system.

When we fall into the delusion of expertise, we become overwhelmed or seduced by knowledge, techniques, or technology. Having expertise is not necessarily wrong, but expertise alone will not make us effective leaders.

The Delusion Of Empathy

The second delusion is the delusion of empathy. Now, having empathy is a good thing. But empathy alone doesn't make us effective leaders. The delusion of empathy is the falsehood that if we only let people know that we understand them and are sensitive to how they feel, then they will follow us.

It's also the false belief that we can overcome inappropriate, unhealthy, or destructive behaviour in others by appealing to reason, fairness, and sensitivity.

A leader doesn't need to feel another person's pain in order to lead them effectively.

Not only is empathy ineffective as a leadership strategy, it may also be detrimental.

Leaders who use empathy as a leadership method often reinforce people in their unhealthy state and don't encourage them to become responsible, mature, and healthy. When people who are immature and unhealthy get our attention and our empathy, they often lose their drive to become healthy and mature.

Of course, good leaders will have empathy. People do want to know that we care for them. They do value leaders who take time to understand them. But simply becoming more empathetic will not make us better leaders. Sometimes as leaders we will have to do things that cause some pain and make people feel uncomfortable. In that case, it's good to be able to say, "this will be unpleasant for you", but we still must lead the people through the painful situation.

The Delusion Of Togetherness

The next delusion is the delusion of togetherness. This is the deception that if we only have enough "togetherness" (that is, consensus) in our people-system, then we will lead people effectively.

In the delusion of togetherness, we simply want people to agree harmoniously and sacrifice their principles for the greater good so that we might achieve some fuzzy consensus about what we should do. Once this is achieved we assume that people will play well together and follow our leadership. But it doesn't happen this way.

Leaders may easily mistake togetherness for unity. Obviously, unity is one of the signs of a healthy people-system. However, unity and togetherness are not the same thing.

Unity is a Spirit-filled force that promotes diversity, maturity, and community among people. Within unity, people can disagree with one another even as they submit to one another out of reverence for Christ, co-operating with one another so that together they achieve good outcomes.

Togetherness may give a false perception of unity. The quest for "togetherness" often becomes a coercive force that compels homogeneity and agreement among people. At its worst, togetherness may actually promote immaturity among people by pressuring people to surrender their personal responsibility to the larger group.

In order to resist the delusion of togetherness, we must have a well-defined sense of being – including our principles, values, and calling – and remain connected to the people-system. We also must encourage other people to have a well-defined sense of their being – in other words, to be mature. If we don't promote this, even in the midst of "togetherness" we may find that we have factions and the loss of community. People who are healthy and mature will work together in ways that promote true unity.

The Delusion Of Position

The final delusion is the delusion of position. This is the lie that if we only have the right position or title, or if we only exert enough power, then we will be an effective leader.

Although we would like to think that this delusion is self-evident, many Christian leaders fall prey to it. We strive after power or position or titles or degrees in order to convince people that we are the ones who should be the leaders. We want them to know that we are qualified to be leaders, so they must follow us. It's so important that we remember what Jesus said in Luke, that if we want to become great then we must become the servant of all.

If we try to lead based on our position or power, then we will always create crises and conflicts of will that will disrupt our people-system. People might try to disguise the conflicts with charm, niceness, or appeals to "fairness", but they will still be harmful. As a leader, Jesus embraced the place of weakness and servanthood. He emptied Himself and took on the form of a servant. We must follow his example if we are to escape the delusion of position.

Dispelling Delusions

As leaders, we must expose these delusions for the deceptions they are. We need to help reset the expectations of our people-system.

We must choose to lead from our identity in Christ as the person God has made us to be. We are leaders by God's calling and by God's design, but our worth as persons doesn't depend on or come from our leadership.

Here is our last leadership dilemma for this course – although by no means the last one you'll face as a leader:

We call these dilemmas "group pitfalls", but our *being* and *doing* as leaders will determine more than anything else whether our people-systems get stuck in them.

Overcoming pitfalls requires a lot of courage and endurance. It requires that we exercise self-control, ensuring that we maintain a healthy connection with the people whom we are leading.

It requires that the love of God for people and our people-system consumes us, so that our self-giving reflects the self-giving of God in his Son, Jesus Christ. It requires that the Spirit of God fills us with his power, so that we can serve as Jesus served.

Transforming Leadership

The purpose of this introduction to Step Seven is to help build and increase the faith of the course participants by identifying how some of the key aspects of our faith as Christians – such as love, faith, the cross, and others – might enable our leadership to become transformative.

Because Christ Is In Us

Genuinely transforming leadership begins with the reality of Christ in us as leaders. As new creations in Christ, our self (being) has been redeemed and renewed. The mystery for us according to Paul in Colossians is that Christ is in us, which gives us the hope of glory.

We May Become Authentically Ourselves As Leaders

Christ in us is the reason we don't have to become like someone else in order to lead. God doesn't want us to become someone else. Christ is in us so that we might become **authentically ourselves** as leaders who are new creations in Christ.

Christ in us gives us real hope that our leadership will bring glory to God. Christ in us also gives us real hope that our leadership will change lives and people-systems. We not only become great leaders but also our leadership will perhaps show Jesus Christ to the world.

Leadership begins with who we are, our being, which has been redeemed and renewed through a living relationship with Jesus Christ. Because of this, as our being grows healthier in Christ we can become stronger leaders.

We Can Develop Abilities To Boost Our Growth And Effectiveness

Because Christ is in us, we can develop several abilities that will boost our growth and effectiveness as leaders. Any Christian can do these things because the Holy Spirit has already given us all we need for life and godliness (see 2 Peter 1:3). Any Christian leader practising these things will grow in leadership impact because Christ is in us.

These abilities are things that will boost everything we do as they flow from our healthy being in Christ. We discuss several of these things in the *Freed To Lead* book, but here I only want to mention three:

First, we must **know ourselves**. We need to know the person that God has created us to be and rejoice in that person. Effective leadership requires knowing who you are and maintaining a high degree of integrity.

Knowing ourselves means that we give up trying to be someone or something other than who we are. God has made each of us unique and given us uniquely important leadership roles. We need to accept that God has designed us to be the leaders we are.

Second, we must **control ourselves**. Self-control is the only biblical form of control. Many leaders lose their leadership in just an instant by losing their self-control in the heat of the moment. Exercising self-control by pausing for a minute or two often makes all the difference between success and failure in any given situation.

Third, we need to **communicate ourselves**. People long to know who we are – our passions, our dreams, our vision. When we choose to communicate ourselves, we engage with the emotional core of people, giving them a sense that they know us and helping them decide to follow us.

This means that we will make ourselves vulnerable. Sometimes we'll get hurt, but people need to get close to us. Vulnerability indicates strength, for only a strong person will have the courage and ability to become vulnerable. The incarnation of Jesus Christ demonstrates this reality most clearly.

Communicating ourselves also means that we connect ourselves with others – their passions, hopes, and dreams. Leading connects our lives with the lives of others so that we go into the future together.

Embracing Christ in us as leaders turbocharges our leadership. Too often we limit our leadership to the realm of perceived possibilities rather than understanding that the presence of Christ in us enables our leadership to achieve more than we might ask or imagine.

We Can Transform Our Leadership Through:

Because of Christ in us, several qualities will transform our leadership and make it transformative as well. These qualities don't replace other aspects of being and doing in leadership, but they enhance and intensify them. These qualities enable us to leave a legacy in the lives of people.

Love

The first quality is **love**. Love is a zealous, self-giving commitment to others for their benefit. This love is not romance, sentimentality, emotionalism, tolerance, indulgence, and similar things. This love is a costly, passionate focus on God's best for others. This love is rooted in the self-giving love of God in Jesus Christ.

Having love recognizes that all people and people-systems have their faults and failures. But love chooses not to focus on these faults and failures. I've heard many leaders secretly (or not so secretly) disparage their city, people-system or people. Without realizing it, they're undermining their leadership effectiveness because they're undermining their love. Love does not focus on that which is ugly but chooses to focus on that which is beautiful.

Having love involves choosing to commit ourselves to others even when it's difficult or not what we'd prefer. I've heard many leaders daydreaming about what their next leadership challenge might be or longing for another person's leadership situation. Without realizing it, they're undermining their leadership effectiveness because they're undermining their love. Love chooses to give itself in a full commitment to the other.

Faith

The second quality is **faith**. Leadership requires faith in God that releases a spirit of adventure which optimizes God's providence. Faith in God enables us to have new perceptions beyond the control of our normal thinking processes. This faith operates at the intersection of risk and reality. The search for safety and certainty are enemies of faith.

All people live and operate by faith. Even atheists have faith, it's just not faith in God. Christian faith is choosing to trust and act, often beyond our natural abilities, based on true knowledge of God and God's ways founded in a relationship with God through Jesus Christ in the power of the Holy Spirit.

We can only have genuine faith as Christians when we have a true knowledge of God and His ways. Our knowledge of God and His ways will only come in relationship with God through Jesus in the power the Holy Spirit. Faith is grounded in God's revelation of Himself in the Bible.

Having a true knowledge of God and His ways based on the Bible enables us to trust Him and then act accordingly. When we do this, God takes us beyond our natural abilities and empowers our leadership with an aspect of Himself that allows our leadership to become more effective in the lives of people.

We need to rescue faith from the common distortions and misrepresentations of faith in the world around us, even among Christians. Faith is not positive thinking, sincere opinions strongly held, emotionalism, blind commitment, tradition, willpower, closed-mindedness, dogmatism, or irrational belief in the face of contrary evidence. These misconceptions of faith undermine the power of faith in our lives.

Faith cherishes uncertainty and keeps us from the deception that we are omniscient. This faith opens us up to the surprises of God's providence that will liberate us from preconceived notions of reality and possibility. This faith gives rise to sanctified imaginations of possibilities within God's kingdom. Such faith acts as a binder of anxiety, especially in the leader.

Embracing The Cross

Power is a major issue in leadership – who has it, who can get it, who benefits from it. The fundamental error that many people make is to think they must get and keep power in order to lead well. People think they need to exert power, even spiritual power, over other people. Jesus showed us another way.

For Christians, the issue of power becomes especially evident when we talk about spiritual warfare. People assume that we must fight demonic spiritual power with Christian spiritual power.

Yet we often forget that Jesus disarmed the principalities and powers through the cross, a symbol of weakness and brokenness, according to Colossians 2:15. If power had ever been the solution, Jesus never would have embraced the cross.

So, the third quality is **embracing the cross**. Jesus' leadership leads straight to the cross. We must be willing to embrace the cross in order to have Christ-like leadership. Embracing the cross means, at least in part:

- Offering up our reputation and good name
- Allowing people to revile us and say all manner of evil against us falsely
- Being excluded and rejected
- Laying down our "weapons"
- Accepting the pain of leadership.

When we embrace the cross, we align ourselves with Jesus' plans and purposes for our lives. We remind ourselves that real leadership does not begin with the exercise of power but with a life surrendered to God in Jesus Christ.

When people see that we are willing to embrace the cross in our own lives, it will help them to have the courage to embrace the cross in their lives.

Perseverance And Endurance

The fourth quality is **perseverance and endurance**. These two words are related but slightly different. Perseverance is steadfastness in doing something despite the difficulty or delay in achieving the beneficial outcome.

Endurance is bearing up under something that is difficult or unpleasant without giving way. Leaders need both perseverance and endurance in order for their leadership to have its full effect.

Modern life gives us an illusion of the quick fix – ATMs, fast-food, supermarkets – which undermines perseverance and endurance. But people develop their personalities, issues and strongholds over months and years. People-systems may even develop their personalities and issues over the course of generations. Significant and lasting change or transformation requires perseverance and endurance.

Sometimes it won't seem like our leadership is making any difference whatsoever. Sometimes we might feel that everything is actually getting worse rather than better. Especially in these times we need to choose to persevere and endure. So often leaders give up just before the battle is won.

Perspective

The final quality is **perspective**. Perspective determines our leadership. Our point of view makes all the difference in whether we see something as beautiful or ugly, as easy or difficult.

Perspective is a function of our reference point. We can choose to change our reference point and therefore choose to change our perspective. Leaders must choose their reference points – and those used by their people-systems – carefully. We might even ask God to give us a new reference point.

As leaders, we must actively seek God's perspective. God's perspective is revealed to us in the Bible. It comes to us in prayer. It may also be revealed through the prophetic. But God's perspective is vital to us as leaders.

When we see the universe as God sees it, we learn two things among others. We learn what a privilege it is that God has chosen us to lead and become agents of transformation in the world that He created. We also learn that our leadership does not depend on our strength and wisdom but on the God who filled us with his Holy Spirit. God himself makes our leadership transformative.

From our perspective, the most significant contribution leaders make is not achieving any particular beneficial outcome. The most significant contribution we make is to the long-term development of people and people-systems so they can adapt, change, prosper, and grow.

We cannot determine our success, effectiveness, or fruitfulness as leaders by simply looking at short-term outcomes and objectives. Leadership success involves transformed people and people-systems, not particular accomplishments.

Many leaders have achieved what they thought of as leadership success only to discover later that ultimately they'd failed in their leadership. Their leadership had achieved numerous accomplishments but left a wake of destroyed lives and destroyed people-systems, often including their own families.

God is a generational God, calling for a long-term perspective. As leaders, we live in the flow of God's holy history. We are an important part of God's history, but that history began before us and will continue long after we cease to lead. We entrust our leadership to this generational God knowing that He will determine the long-term transformative impact of our leadership.

The challenge for us is to lead from the perspective of the legacy we would like to leave, knowing that, as Isaiah reminds us, our God is the one who declares the end from the beginning. The legacy that we leave in the lives of people and people-systems is what will endure long after we are gone.

The Steps To Freedom For Leaders

The objective of the ministry component of the course, *The Steps To Freedom For Leaders*, is to enable participants to identify and resolve footholds of the enemy that might be holding them back as leaders and also to continue to identify areas where their belief system might be faulty so that they can go on to renew their minds.

WORSHIP

- Choose a song that celebrates the salvation of God.
- Read Psalm 37:37–40.
- Thank God for what you have learned or how you have grown during the course.
- Surrender your leadership role to God as an act of taking refuge in Him.

How Does The Away Day Work?

For groups using *Freed To Lead* on a weekly basis, we recommend planning a day away at the end of the course so that the group might go through *The Steps To Freedom For Leaders*.

Any location with a suitable amount of peace and quiet would work for an away day. Many churches simply choose their own fellowship hall or similar facilities. Other churches might decide to opt for a retreat centre, or even another church premises. Regardless of where you choose, it should be convenient and accessible for your group members.

You will need facilities to show the DVD and enough space for people to spread out and spend time on their own with God. Some may prefer to work in pairs, encouraging one another through the Steps in which case you will need to make allowance for that.

We envisage that you will provide some opening worship and perhaps a very short focus from God's Word but then the DVD will facilitate the rest of the process. It provides a brief introduction for each one of the Steps and leads people through the opening prayers as a group. It then pauses automatically for participants to "do business" with God. At this point they should spread out around the room or around the retreat centre, coming back together at the time you specify to resume the process.

Note that Step Seven has a longer introduction of about 20 minutes that also serves as a closing reflection for the whole course. There are notes for this in the Participant's Guide on pages 129–132.

We would encourage you to plan plenty of time for the day. We have provided two suggested time plans overleaf, either of which you might adapt for the use of your group.

The first time plan is envisaged especially for larger groups or groups where the participants do not know one another well. It provides slightly more time for talking and getting to know one another in the earlier portions of the Steps.

The second time plan is for smaller groups or groups where people know each other quite well. They may require less time at the start of the away day and more time on some of the later Steps.

Standard Timing For Churches And Larger Groups

10.00 – 10.30	Welcome and worship
10.30 – 11.00	Opening Prayer and Declaration (with Discussion Questions)
11.00 – 11.15	Break
11.15 – 12.00	Step One – Embracing Our Identity In Christ
12.00 – 12.30	Step Two – Forgiveness In Leadership
12.30 – 13.30	Lunch
13.30 – 14.15	Step Three – Overcoming Anxiety And Reactivity In Leadership
14.15 – 14.45	Step Four – Embracing Our Leadership Responsibility
14.45 – 15.00	Break
15.00 – 15.30	Step Five – Money, Sex, And Power In Leadership
15.30 – 16.00	Step Six – Renouncing Pride, Defensiveness, And Selfish Ambition In Leadership
16.00 – 16.20	Introduction to Step Seven
16.20 – 16.50	Step Seven – Choosing Faith For Leading, with closing prayer and declaration
16.50 – 17.00	Closing worship and praying for one another

Alternate Timing For Smaller Groups And Groups Who Know One Another Well

10.00 – 10.30	Welcome and worship
10.30 – 10.45	Opening Prayer and Declaration (with Discussion Questions)
10.45 – 11.15	Step One – Embracing Our Identity In Christ
11.15 – 11.30	Break
11.30 – 12.00	Step Two – Forgiveness In Leadership
12.00 – 12.45	Step Three – Overcoming Anxiety And Reactivity In Leadership
12.45 – 13.30	Lunch
13.30 – 14.00	Step Four – Embracing Our Leadership Responsibility
14.00 – 14.45	Step Five – Money, Sex, And Power in Leadership
14.45 – 15.00	Break
15.00 – 15.45	Step Six – Renouncing Pride, Defensiveness, And Selfish Ambition In Leadership
15.45 – 16.05	Introduction to Step Seven
16.05 – 16.30	Step Seven – Choosing Faith For Leading, with closing prayer and declaration
16.30 – 17.00	Closing worship and praying for One Another

About The Authors

Rod Woods

Dr. Rod Woods leads as the senior minister of the City Temple, a polycultural Christian church in the heart of London. He and his wife, Karen, have served churches in the United States and the United Kingdom.

They have also worked with several international ministries, including Freedom in Christ Ministries (where Rod serves on the UK Board) and HarvestNet International. They seek to serve as catalysts for renewal throughout the Body of Christ.

Steve Goss

Having embarked upon a career in marketing eventually starting his own mail order business, Steve has no idea how he ended up working full-time for Freedom In Christ Ministries, writing Christian books, presenting DVD courses and speaking at events around the UK and internationally. He and Zoë started Freedom In Christ's UK office in 1999 thinking they would "give it Friday afternoons" and it all went from there...

His passions are discipleship and unity. He co-wrote (with Neil Anderson) *The Freedom In Christ Discipleship Course* which quickly became a best-seller. It has now been used by well over 250,000 people in the UK and been translated into around a dozen languages. He became Freedom In Christ's International Director in 2012 and now spearheads its work around the world.

Selected Bibliography

Neil T. Anderson. *The Bondage Breaker*. Oxford: Monarch Books, 2002.

_____. *Steps To Freedom In Christ*. Oxford: Monarch Books, 2009.

_____. *Victory Over The Darkness*. Oxford: Monarch Books, 2002.

Neil T. Anderson and Steve Goss. *Freedom in Christ Leader's Guide: A 13 Week Discipleship Course for Every Christian*. Oxford: Monarch Books, 2009.

Steve Goss, Rich Miller, and Jude Graham. *The Grace Course Leader's Guide*. Oxford: Monarch Books, 2012.

George Barna. *The Power of Vision*. Ventura: Gospel Light, 2009.

Stephen M.R Covey. *The Speed of Trust: The One Thing that Changes Everything*. London: Simon & Schuster, 2006.

Edwin H Friedman. *A Failure of Nerve: Leadership in the Age of the Quick Fix*. New York: Church Publishing, 2007.

Steve Goss. *Break Free, Stay Free: Don't Let the Past Hold You Back*. Oxford: Monarch Books, 2008.

_____. *Free to Be Yourself: Enjoy Your True Nature in Christ*. Oxford: Monarch Books, 2008.

_____. *Win the Daily Battle: Resist and Stand Firm in God's Strength*. Oxford: Monarch Books, 2008.

_____. *The You God Planned: Don't Let Anything or Anyone Hold You Back*. Oxford: Monarch Books, 2008.

Daniel Kahneman. *Thinking, Fast and Slow*. London: Penguin Books, 2011.

Bob Sorge. *Loyalty: The Reach of the Noble Heart*. Lee's Summit: Oasis House, 2004.

Peter L Steinke. *Congregational Leadership in Anxious Times: Being Calm and Courageous No Matter What*. Herndon: The Alban Institute, 2006.

_____. *Healthy Congregations: A Systems Approach*. Herndon: The Alban Institute, 2006.

_____. *How Your Church Family Works: Understanding Congregations as Emotional Systems*. Herndon: The Alban Institute, 2006.

Philip Zimbardo. *The Lucifer Effect: How Good People Turn to Evil*. London: Ryder, 2007.